Dear ~~Shalom~~

Love for all,
Peace for all,
Tolerance for all,
and above all else,
Passion for all!

Irene

Dear Irene,

"May your book inspire us to rise above the narrow confines of our individualistic concerns, to the broader concerns of all humanity. May you inspire us to bring passion, not only between the sheets of life but also directly into our experiences with other people. May you inspire us to remember as humans, we are relational beings. May you inspire us to come face to face with core human experiences and may you empower us to allow clarity and freedom to illuminate our relationships with others."

Keep pushing the pen!! Chaim

Chaim Cohen serves on the Board of Directors of numerous Civil Society organizations that promote human rights, interfaith understanding, nonviolence, and social and environmental justice. He is also on the steering committee of the United Nations group that supports and coordinates Civil Society and governmental representatives from all regions of the world in advancing the cause of peace and justice in the Middle East. Chaim Cohen recently keynoted at the United Nations International meeting in support of Israeli-Palestinian Peace, where he focused on the significance of peace in the Middle East for the advancement of the dialogue between cultures and civilizations.

Edited by Margaret Heslop

Copyright ©
February 25, 2009
ISBN 978-0-9812676-0-9

Published by Irene Brautigam and Jennifer Warwick

Printed in U.S.A. by Herald Printing Company,
New Washington, OH

All names of people in this book have been changed to protect
their privacy, except that of Irene Brautigam.

Passion Between the Sheets of Life

Book One

An Open Heart

Written by
Irene Brautigam

I dedicate this book to JC and want to thank him for his patience with me, for his depth of understanding human nature and for the amazing passion that he has for his music and for me. It is through his understanding of passion that I have been able to better understand my own. Without him in my life, this book may never have been written and this book is the fruit of our passion.

I also dedicate this book to my mother and my father, Barbara and Paul, who taught me much of what I know about having passion in one's life and in all things we do. I also dedicate this to my daughter, Jennifer, and my son, David, who through their births and their belonging to me, softened the touch of my passion and yet gave it strength.

Last, but certainly not least, I want to thank all those people I have met and have crossed paths with in my life and in particular those who have been a thorn in my side or a boulder in my path, because from you, I think I may have learned the most.

Irene

AUTHOR'S NOTE

It was difficult for me to reread many of the emails that went into this book and I did much better with a box of tissues beside me and a glass of wine. It was a difficult time in my life and was not one I wanted to revisit. From the early stages of the relationship, I felt it was vital that I continue to write in spite of the fact Jimmy was eager to receive them. They allowed me to maintain the connection with him and to somehow preserve my sanity. It quickly became my daily journal and I truly believed there was something very special about this man.

In hindsight, many of the emails were written to create a façade in preparation for another heartbreak which I anticipated around the corner. Much of my persona was that of an eccentric. No facet of my life at the time presented stability, including this new relationship. I had just failed at a marriage. I now entered a career where I was taught that 80% fail and, true to my nature, I continued to forge ahead.

I remember being told there are two types of people in the world. There are those who walk through the swamp to reach the other side and then there are those who will always take the bridge. I am blessed to say most of my life has been spent on the bridge. This, at least, is my perception.

The one thing that will always remain a constant with me will be the truth. I have strived to maintain the integrity and truth of this story without jeopardizing the people I love. I have taught my children that at some point a story may need a form of embellishment and this should be considered acceptable.

I could not "white wash" these emails and move from the truth because the term is discriminatory in itself and this is a place I will never go, regardless of the consequence. My whole upbringing and background would never allow this.

I remember sitting with my mother and grandmother when I was fifteen years old and in Germany for the first time. It was only the three of us and my mother asked my grandmother if she still had sex with my grandfather. My grandmother was in her late seventies at the time and my grandfather, in his early eighties. I will never forget my grandmother's response. She looked at her daughter and said, "I would love to, but he just can't anymore". The openness and honesty of the question and answer is how I strive to live my life.

I enlisted my own daughter's help with this book and this lasted about three days. Once the emails became too personal she declined further assistance, which was understandable. It does not negate the fact she and I, as with my son, have maintained a very close relationship throughout our lives. There was never a topic of discussion between us that was considered taboo, regardless of how painful.I told my daughter tonight, she needed to take a step back from this book and her personal ties to it. I promised her I would remove those discussions between her and I that would cause her grief and I have done so. I wanted her to try and view it on a broader scope and not sexual in nature because this is not what the book is about. I told her never to view sex between two people who love each other, as a disgusting act. All love, kindness and caring in this world must start in the home and not elsewhere.

I asked her if this circle of life should begin in the home and move outwards from there or would it operate better in the reverse? When two people love each other enough to have children and these children are raised in love, they will go out into the world with this love in their hearts. These same children will become the loving and caring adults that the world desperately needs.

Many parents have taken themselves out of the equation of child rearing for one reason or another and it is now left to society. Society, unfortunately, is ill equipped to raise a world full of loving and caring people. To verify the truth to this statement, we only need to turn on the news today or to skip a flat stone on water and watch which way the ripples go.

Irene

P.S. Sometimes it is much more difficult to live events than it is to write about them. I only hope it is easier to read. The next of this series will give more laughter.

Part 1
Reconnecting

Chapter 1

Canmore is a beautiful and diverse small mountain community, nestled in the heart of the luxurious blue Canadian Rockies. It is located just outside of Banff National Park. Over the years we have become an internationally renowned tourist destination and each year people from all over the world flock to our mountains for not only its scenic wonder and wildlife, but also for its numerous sports opportunities, such as skiing and climbing.

I was raised in these mountains from the age of six months. My parents and older brother, Morgan, emigrated from Germany in 1952. My father wanted something better for his family than what war torn Europe offered at the time. After a brief stay in Calgary and Drumheller, they wound up settling in 1954 in the Bow Valley , where I was born. I, Irene Katharina Brautigam, was the first child born in Canada. My younger sister, Rosie, was born two years later in Banff.

Throughout my childhood and into my teens, money was sparse and much of our spare time was spent picking wild berries, fishing, collecting and skipping stones. Our first two homes in these mountains were small two room shacks; the second one my parents bought. Both consisted only of a kitchen and one bedroom. There was a small porch on the front and the bathroom was outside.

The house seemed large to me and when my grandmother finally came to live with the six of us, we all piled onto bunk beds my father had made out of lumber from the dump and yet it still seemed big enough for all of us. Years later this house was turned into our chicken coop.

We bought our first refrigerator for this second house. Unfortunately, it wouldn't work for over a year because there wasn't enough power running into the home to accommodate it. For the time being, my mother continued to rely on meats packed in lard and stone crocks which were buried outside, underground.

Water was brought by pails from the Bow River to the house and later from a pump and well in the yard. Our baths were taken in a small round metal tub set out in the middle of the kitchen floor and my mother or grandmother would heat the water on the coal stove. My sister was first in the bath and my brother was the last. I never knew when my parents and grandmother bathed and it must have been after my bedtime.

I was five years old when we finally moved into the new five bedroom house my mother and father had built with their own hands from the ground up. Much of the building materials came from the dump including used nails which had to be hammered straight. We now lived in the largest house in town.

The years that followed were still financially very difficult. The work for my father was never steady and both my parents' health suffered from the years of hard work. My father spent six months in a Calgary sanatorium with tuberculosis and it was a miracle he survived.

Things improved after he came home and life became normal again. For many years our house was a revolving door for people or families who needed shelter or a place to live for awhile. My mother tended a vegetable garden which was sufficient for the year to feed our family and more. Food was always plentiful with our chickens, rabbits, wild game, the fish we caught and the pig we bought from the farmer once a year. We were more than happy and satisfied.

Chapter 2

Throughout these years, I was especially close to my sister, Rosie. We shared the same bedroom for years. I led her in prayer most of those nights while we were growing up. While I rubbed her back and tried to help her doze off, prayers were always the last thing we did before she went to sleep. All through high school, I dreamed of becoming a psychologist and helping people deal with their misery. I was astutely aware of the fact that most of this was self induced and could easily be fixed. The other career option for me was to travel the world and make an attempt at becoming the next Mother Teresa (MT). Before the end of school, our family went to Europe to finally meet my mother's side of the family. In 1970, I went to Expo Japan with other southern Alberta students. By the time I graduated from high school, my sister refused to continue with her schooling. That summer she ran away from home for a few days. I found her in a cabin in Banff, smoking pot with a bunch of hippies. When I asked her to come home with me, she sneered and told me to "F…off, you don't know 'where it's at'". She was only fourteen at the time and I remember how this really hurt me, as we had been so close. Here I was being told to "F…off", by someone whom I loved dearly; I didn't know anything and, therefore, what right did I have to judge and tell someone what they should do with their lives. I gave up my notions of a career in psychology and decided I needed to find out WHERE exactly it was I should be. By this time in my life, I became the "white sheep" of the family. Trouble seemed to find both Rosie and Morgan, while I was only going to school, working and travelling. A great deal of resentment grew between us, as a result.

Once I graduated, on numerous occasions, I tried living in the city, but the lure of the mountains always managed to draw me back. From the late 60's and throughout the 70's, I travelled most parts of the world and found beauty everywhere I went. Three months was the longest I could stay in these faraway places, before returning to my tranquil and picturesque home.

I opened the first furniture store here in 1980. I met my husband, John, when he was sent to interview me about an airport proposal I had been working on. We married two years later and I remember telling him that as a Catholic, divorce would never be an option for me. If I ever caught him playing around, he would have one of two options-a rolling pin or the frying pan.

For many years, my only concerns were my husband and the raising and nurturing of our two children, Julianna and Danny. Even after the store sold, I was too busy to share a quick cup of coffee with a friend and my home/ work schedule eliminated the last of my old friendships. I retired to raise my two children, to run a "Bed and Breakfast" and to manage our properties. Like my parents before me, I became the general fixer, maker, builder and renovator of the household. I looked back on my store days as an easier time in my life.

Chapter 3

Cephus Jambala and I met at Benny's, a new night spot that recently opened and featured a three piece live band every Friday and Saturday night. Cephus was the keyboard player in the trio. He was originally from St. Vincent and by age fifteen he had started playing in the top bands of the country.. His musical career began with the big bands of the era. His father was in Education and, with pressure from him, he followed in his footsteps and became a teacher. This lasted two years while he still played evenings and weekends. For the summer break, he went to Barbados to play in a Jazz band and he never went back to teaching.

He moved to Canada in the late 60s when he was twenty-four. Chuck, the owner of Benny's, was originally from the U.S. and Greg was from Trinidad and also lived in Canada since the 60s. Greg and Cephus played together down East in a number of bands and both eventually moved out West in the early 70s. They were good friends and they played together fairly regularly, for nearly forty years.

The three played a wonderful variety of music, including Jazz and the Blues. Canmore rarely offered the type of music I preferred and this was a nice treat. It was easy to see why it became such a popular night spot.

My husband was working as a realtor and Benny's was the venue for various functions throughout the year. His female co-workers went out regularly for girls' night and I would often join them.

During these visits I would go outside to have a smoke on the deck. Coincidentally, Cephus would either already be out there or he would join me soon after. Cephus, however, did not smoke. I did not look at other men and, therefore, I never bothered to remember his name. He became "Larry" to me for a number of years.

Our conversations were very casual and never about anything in particular, except my skills at the time as cook, baker and candlestick maker. From career woman, I had become the ultimate domestic. On these occasions, we never discussed personal issues. In fact I tried to line him up with a girlfriend of mine who was in need of a good man. He gracefully declined and she really wasn't looking anyway.

Two years later, my husband left me after eighteen years of marriage and I found myself separated with two teenage children. We both have our versions of what caused the separation, but I am only responsible for my own. A year after the separation, I lost about thirty pounds and, as a result, I gained an entire new wardrobe that made me feel good about myself. I made many new friends and I spent the summer dancing with them until the wee hours of the morning.

Chapter 4

My parents invited me to Sammy's fiftieth birthday party at Running Bull's, a place they frequented. Running Bull's was the largest Western bar in Banff that featured nightly live entertainment and also VLTS. My mother and father , while in their eighties, are still enjoying the nightly entertainment and the VLTS. I will be happy if my mother passes away with her head on the slot machine and my father on the dance floor. They worked hard all their lives and they deserve to enjoy their retirement in the ways they want.

The first person I saw standing at the top of the stairs was Cephus. I had no idea they would be playing that night. It was almost a year since we last saw each other. We greeted one another and the first words out of my mouth expressed that John and I had separated. He looked at me, with his friendly eyes, and said, "I'll catch you later."

I worked the room, trying to find familiar faces in the crowd. I was also looking for a new face I may be interested in. I reached the point where I was happy with the new me and I focused on having fun, instead of looking for someone else to make me happy. I spent time trying to line up a guy with a nice young woman and this didn't work. None of the men were possible candidates for me, other than Cephus, and I was happy to see him.

I danced and sang endlessly to Cephus's arranged rendition of the Supremes and it was absolutely brilliant. At the end of their set, Cephus was sitting at the band table when I approached him and asked him to dance. I had nothing planned other than dancing and was under the impression that menopause had taken the life out of sex for me. I had dried up and would have been too embarrassed to admit it. We wound up spending the next few precious hours dancing together as if we had danced together for years. I felt like I was in heaven and wondered if the slight ache in my groin was from the dancing.

My parents were not very happy when I told them to drive home without me and that I would be leaving with Cephus. As we headed out the door, a woman from Banff, to whom I was not acquainted, remarked what a wonderful couple we made. I jokingly told Cephus he could drop me off on the highway by Canmore and he wouldn't have to go out of his way to see me home.

At the end of the evening, he drove me to my door and we talked for quite awhile. For the first time in many years, I discovered an urge to kiss someone. This urge took me by surprise and I felt like a school girl with a crush. I felt I had to seize the opportunity and steal a kiss. I had no idea this one kiss would be so delicious and so addictive that it made the flood gates open.

Chapter 5

Monday, October 16, 2006 12:55 P.M.
Subject: Message in a bottle......Sort of

Hi Irene,

I know that this is a business email address so I won't get personal, but it certainly was nice to see you at Sammy's do on Saturday night and to spend a little time with you (outside of the club setting).....we should do that again.

If you have a personal email address, please send it to me so we can connect......Hope your busy Sunday schedule was successful.

> Keep in touch
>
> Your admirer
>
> Larry.....oops (lol)
>
> Cephus

Sent: Wednesday, October 18, 2006 5:18 P.M.
Subject: Re: Message in a bottle....Sort of

Hello Cephus

I can't remember the last time I had so much fun! Motown was always one of my favourites and the girls did such a terrific job. I couldn't sit down or stop singing and I felt like I'd died and gone to heaven. I do love to dance especially to tunes I can sing along to. The only unfortunate thing is I had a couple of martinis too many. I would like to apologize for throwing myself at you when you were so kind in taking me home. This is not something I have done in at least twenty-five years, but it has happened before.

I also enjoyed dancing with you and wished I had had the opportunity for it not to end so soon after it began. I would love to do it again. Let me know when it would work for you.

My email address at home is 123456@yahoo.ca. You can send emails there or here to work. It doesn't matter; however, there have been problems with sending and receiving here. There are six computers in the office and I don't know if they are overworked and tired, but too many times I have trouble getting emails in and out or going missing altogether.

I still haven't arranged a date with my new gang of friends for what has become my annual birthday celebration at Benny's. I would imagine it should be in the next couple of weeks. Don't feel you need to wait for then to give me a call.

I do have to go now. It's been a huge week, with two offers going conditional.....and I received my first pay cheque in ten years that actually had my name on it. Time to celebrate.

Talk to you soon....Irene

While I was busy, thinking of me, and a new beginning in my romantic life, a tragedy struck. It made me stop and think about the value of each day and how each day must be taken one at a time. We have to make certain we love and do our best each and every day of our lives. The day of this next email, a forty year old co-worker, her husband, the husband's uncle and wife were all killed in a head on collision.Sent: October 20, 2006 1:48 P.M.

Subject: Re: Message in a bottle....Sort of

Hello Cephus

I could really use someone to talk to this weekend. We just lost a forty year old co-worker and her husband in a head on collision by Revelstoke. They were going away for the weekend to celebrate her fortieth birthday and left their two young children at home with the grandparents. I have been on floor duty this morning and it has been extremely difficult for everyone in the office to continue as if nothing has happened. I am just heading out to see some clients and then I will call it a day. She was a truly wonderful person and they are leaving behind two very lost souls. Hope to talk to you over the weekend.

Irene

Sent: October 20, 2006 3:59 P.M.
Subject: Hi there......

Hi Irene,

I got both your messages and was about to reply to you on the first one when I got your next....Now that's not good news at all. What is it about that Revelstoke junction area?......I lost a friend of mine on a motorbike there a couple of years ago...You have my deepest sympathy of course.

I'll be in DMF later to play tonight. I have to get there at a reasonable time to set up my gear....I'll give you a shout by phone and see if we can hook up. At least I can give you a shoulder to lean on for a while......

Take care.......Later

Cephus

Cephus came to visit that Friday night after he finished playing at Benny's. I remember being excited about this first visit and yet the sadness and cloud of Mary's death hung over the evening. On this first visit, I began to listen to his stories. I became enthralled with his wonderful storytelling, and I was also amused by his hand gestures and the intonations of his voice. I found his laugh and smile infectious. His speech was rapid and, with his Vincentian accent, I had to really pay attention or he would have lost me.

He began to tell me stories of his childhood back in Chateaubelair, St. Vincent. For the first ten years of his life, Cephus lived in this small fishing village with his sister and mother. On the other hand, his father, lived and taught in the capital of Kingstown, which was a four hour boat ride. His father would often come home for the weekend. In preparation for these visits, his mother used to spend hours fussing with her hair. I suppose it was back then when Cephus began to pay attention to the habits and routines of women. He also found it interesting that his mother, who never drank coffee, would make such a fuss over the choice of beans to be used on the weekend when his father was coming home. Cephus knew he only drank cocoa in the city. By the time Cephus was eleven, he moved to the city to attend a private school and live with his father.

During the course of our evening, many times he purposefully slowed his speech down and then suddenly he stopped altogether to reflect. All the while he would hold his index finger, suspended in mid air, a hair away from the skin on my arm. When I saw the finger coming the first time, I almost flinched and wanted to know what he would do with it. I almost burst into laughter when it stopped, just shy of touching me and it stayed there. Suddenly, I felt a bolt of electricity go straight from my arm to between my legs. I think he knew the effect it produced in women.

By the time we said good night I realized I never met a storyteller like this. It reminded me of my own skills, but different, of course. Through the years of raising my two children, I knew it wasn't necessarily the story, but how it was told that made the difference. I tried to teach my children these principles. It was in this way that Cephus first drew my attention. In a way, I suppose I felt like a child again and I was truly entertained by this unpretentious and gentle person's musical speech.

Chapter 6

Sent: October 24, 2006 2:25 P.M.
Subject: Message in a bottle

Hi Cephus

Thank you for running up to Canmore to see me last Friday and to lend your shoulder, although I didn't really take advantage of it. It is awkward with children in the house. My son, Danny, wanted to apologize for not coming upstairs to meet you. I talked to him the next morning to ask why he was unkind and he was under the impression that you were not in the house yet. He thought I wanted him to wait upstairs for you to arrive and couldn't figure out why.

It was good to hear a bit of your life history. I do have one complaint to make. You failed to continue the story to the present. I feel like you left out an important part and whether you are currently involved with someone else or are married. It is important. The last thing I would want to do is hop into someone else's bed.

Twice now you have left me thinking what it would be like to be lying next to your naked body which I find is totally unfair. What you may not realize is that it's been over a year since John left; I now know I have not died sexually. I have managed to stay focused on my new career and lived like a eunuch this past year and never gave it a second thought. Now things have changed and it appears, for the past two weeks, I am catching myself thinking these impure thoughts of you. It could be they aren't impure and just natural. Some days I still feel married and I will have to get over that.

All of a sudden I feel like I am twenty again...okay.....twenty-nine. I was never one to hesitate and always went after what I wanted. The only thing holding me back is if John ever found out it could wind up costing me more than I am prepared to lose. No one likes to lose in life. The children and I have talked about our rendezvous and

19

they are quite happy to know that their mother is alive and actually quite normal. That doesn't mean they would be pleased to wake up one day and find me in bed with you.

Well, enough for now. What are your views on this subject? It could be you are totally not interested, especially after that kiss. You really must promise me one thing. Please allow me time to brush my teeth next time. I have been told often by my non-smoking ex what it is like to kiss a smoker. That is, of course, if there is a next time. I have to make a trip into Calgary very soon to pick up a number of things. I would be willing to meet you in the city, if that suits you. Let me know.

Irene

Sent: October 27, 2006 10:18 A.M.
Subject: Here's that bottle again....

Hi Irene,

Just got back into town last night after a little jaunt to Montreal for a couple of days....Kind of hectic, but sometimes that's the nature of the session business...but I also got to spend a bit of time with my son at McGill and also see my older sister for a brief spell.

You are very welcome for the shoulder (that you didn't take advantage of)....but the circumstances and the environs just weren't there, of course...and then the tension of the kids....the aura of John....etc. but it still was nice.....

We were still talking about me when your daughter, Julianna, came in last week....but to answer your question, I am not married. I never did re-marry after my only marriage collapsed in 1972. I think I was just too pissed off and I have always found an emotional solace in music. I've had a few relationships and many of them good and two wonderful children that I raised from two of those relationships besides the two children from my marriage. Currently I am not involved. Maybe I've become too much a cynic or I have worn out my tolerance for the emotional complications of intimacy but I still get attracted to the opposite sex. I was very attracted to you when we met awhile ago, which I thought was a waste of time or just lust for

20

someone's wife, which was a no-go as you inferred…back then.

What's so special about being 29? Less mental and emotional baggage I guess…..a chance to be carefree. You seem like a "go for it" person, anyway.

Hope the funerals of Mary and Darren were not too heavy around the office and the town. Life is so short. I'll give you a dingle on the weekend. I think we have lots to jaw about.

Take care,
Cephus

Sent: October 27, 2006 4:25 P.M.
Subject: P.S. ###

Hi Irene,

Just a quick P.S.….

My easiest number…….cell is 403-123-4659

Talk to you soon
Cephus

Chapter 7

Cephus arrived around 12:30 A.M. that Friday night after his gig. During his visits, we would talk until around 3:00 A.M. before he would head back to the city. I say "we" would talk but, in fact, he was doing most of the talking. I assumed that because he had spent a lifetime on stage, he did not have the opportunity to converse as frequently as the rest of us. Maybe this was the reason he could go on and on for hours, but I enjoyed it. I spent a lifetime in sales and I was used to doing all the talking. With Cephus, I cherished a time to listen, for a change.

I enjoy listening to others in both my career and home life and I viewed these stories as gifts of knowledge and experience. While listening to Cephus, I felt like I was allowed to walk a mile in his shoes. I was thankful he was willing to share a piece of himself with me. By the next visit, I could hardly contain my anticipation-he was not going to leave in the middle of the night. I hoped he would stay until morning and I looked forward to what would come between us.

I recall the evening so well.

We were sitting in the music room, listening to more stories of his past. He started that night with a story about when he first moved to Canada. Cephus followed his childhood sweetheart to Toronto where she had moved and they had married. Unfortunately, after two years the marriage fell apart. He suspected she actually loved another and this really soured him to "bands of gold", but he did stay faithful throughout his marriage. It took him the next twenty years to recover from that experience. He had another relationship with a woman who wanted a child and she gave birth to his third daughter, Allison. Years later, he lived with a woman for five years and his only son, Jordon, was born. Both children lived with him, although

Jordon was in Montreal studying music and Allison worked in Calgary.

When he first moved to Canada from the Caribbean, he frequented music stores in order to practise daily on the ivories. It was at this time he discovered his first elevator and its music. Prior to this, he had only heard the soft music in films and, after this first ride, he sought out elevators, only with pencil and paper, to write down the notes to the songs he didn't know.

It was on these joyrides that he noticed women generally found it necessary to push the button even though the light was lit. He wondered if they thought the elevator actually moved quicker as a result. From these elevator excursions, he decided that women, who pushed the button twice, were also most likely prone to repeatedly push the buttons of loved ones.

I noticed his stories would often go from one period in time to another without the completion of the first story. His stories wandered from the elevator and his practices on the piano, and then he went back to the Caribbean and his early childhood and how he actually started on the violin.

When Cephus was five, his older sister received a violin for her birthday and he was envious of her. He picked it up and he started to play it. His parents were in awe and they quickly realized that he was musically gifted and soon he had a violin of his own. By the age of ten, his parents sent him for a year to study at a music school in England. When he reached puberty, he noticed that women paid more attention to the piano player and he quickly set the violin aside.

By the end of the evening his story revolved around Cooler's, one of only two night spots in Canmore in the early 80's. He was playing in a band, called Ebony, at the time. A woman in the audience sent the manager to invite him over for a drink. As a musician his whole life, he had found that it was common for women, especially after drinking, to want to take a member of the band home.

He recalled how this woman had owned a gift shop in Canmore. I told Cephus there were only two gift shops here at that time. One was owned by a Dutch couple and the other was owned by my best friend. He sat there and began to think of her name, telling me that his excellent memory was something he got from his father. The next thing I knew he blurted out the name, "Perkins", but he couldn't remember her first name. I hit him with a pillow and I told him that this was my girlfriend's married name. I filled in his blank with "Maggie". He told me that the evening had ended with my girlfriend and him back at her house.

This took me by surprise. For years I couldn't figure out why men appeared to be so enthralled with blonds, blue eyes and big boobs. My girlfriend had just separated from her first husband. She had two children and she still managed to have three marriage proposals that first year of her separation. The last one she accepted.

I was always envious of the number of men she had seemed to attract in her life; while my main focus had always been on my work. I was approaching thirty with not a soul in sight who interested me. I was fussy and I did ignore opportunities that came my way, but somehow I still felt hard done by. I had no one to blame, but myself. I was the one who had decided to open the furniture store at age twenty-six and was back at work six or seven days a week. I certainly never made time for a serious relationship.

I remember feeling somewhat repulsed and jealous about his rendezvous with my best friend. I was very attracted to him and my best friend reached first base before I did. It wasn't important who initiated this. It happened. I let him drive home that night, thinking if I had any self respect I would not see him again.

Chapter 8

Ultimately, I put my feelings aside and he stayed the next night. The past is the past and it cannot be changed. We need to learn to live with it and get on with life and I was happy that I had changed my mind. I discovered lubricants were definitely not going to be necessary and I decided to go with the flow of this new relationship.

Sent: October 30, 2006 11:50 A.M.
Subject: Calgary trip planned for Irene

Hi Cephus

I hope you made it back into the city yesterday in one piece. The roads were surely not in a good state, but at least you didn't have to leave in the middle of the night. Thank God for that and for more than one reason. I am sooooo thankful as the evening turned out to be phenomenal and not in my wildest dreams did I expect that. It did, however, prove to be difficult for me to wrap my mind around work yesterday afternoon. I could barely wait for closing at 5:00 P.M. and I left a little early. I know I should be satisfied with yesterday, but maybe I am trying to make up for lost time. Sometimes we should avoid over analyzing situations and circumstances and go with the moment.

I did manage to get an email off to my girlfriend this morning so I am curious to know what she thinks of all this. I can imagine she will be surprised. Anyway, I am planning my week (great organizer) and I think I can make it into the city on Wednesday afternoon. Though I wanted to check your schedule first.. All weekend I was trying to remember when I actually had had a full day off and I don't think I have had one since I started this new career in June. Needless to say, I am way overdue. I haven't put my name down for anymore office duty this week. So right now I am pretty flexible as to which days.

Let me know what would work for you, if anything. If you are planning to be away this week, I will still have to go into the city. Let me know.

Irene

Sent: October 31, 2006 1:54 P.M.
Subject: Hi there……

Hi Irene,

I just got your call and went to my mailbox on another computer here…..I've been here in Turner Valley since yesterday before the rush hour and trying to lay down some tracks.

Yes, I made it back to Calgary in one piece on Sunday although the roads were quite wintery and all along the way I kept hoping that Julianna would make it back in good shape too as there were a lot of cars in the ditch heading west.

Saturday night was wonderful in spite of the initial uncertainty. At least we don't have to deal with that again, I hope….next time we could be more relaxed.

Wednesday or Thursday would be ok. We should be able to hook up. I've got to get this session done today and get back to the city later.

Will talk to you later.

Take care.
Cephus

Part 2

The Hook

Chapter 9

Sent: October 31, 2006 6:57 P.M.
Subject: Re: Hi there.....

I hope you don't mind this large print, remember I need reading glasses. No uncertainty here....do I look like a stupid woman? I haven't orgasmed like that for a very, very long time! It isn't just about the sex, you know. There have been other opportunities since, you know who, left.

This summer I met a guy, I called my stalker. I had mistakenly given him a hug after a party and he took it personal. The next thing I knew he was parking in front of my house all the time or where I work. I finally got rid of him after he insisted on me showing him a house when he had no intentions of buying one. I didn't want him in my car and I let him know that. He hasn't been a problem since.

I had to set up appointments with clients tomorrow. As I mentioned on the phone, I can't make it in tomorrow. When you didn't respond to my e-mail, I thought one of two things. Either you only check them once a week or you have a heart condition and wouldn't be able to handle another intimate rendezvous with me. I was hoping it was the first.

I have been very busy since Sunday morning. I decided the best way to handle this affair is the way I have always dealt with issues in my life. First, I had a long discussion with my parents about it yesterday.

They know you and I have seen each other three weekends in a row. Of all the people they have ever met in this life, they know me best. They know I have not had sex for over a year. The first thing my mother did was to give me a smirk, as if to say she knew we hopped into bed. I never did tell them, but they do know me well.

My father, on the other hand, is a little slower because of his hearing. All he could say was that I should be careful not to get hurt because not many people know musicians in the valley as well as he does. All he said was, "you know, Irene, the women they are with in the pubs, are usually not their wives, and they tend to have women in every port".

My mother must have known last week what was going to happen. She never wants to go to DMF, but she phoned me and asked if she was still invited to this delayed birthday party of mine. This is very strange behaviour for her, seeing as how there are no VLTS there.

When I went home Julianna Forest, the twenty-two year old living with us, and I got into a conversation about separated and divorced parents and how they also need a sex life. I believe I initiated it with something about how children assume parents, regardless of age, never have sex and this is the only way children wish to view their parents. They may share the same bed, but they NEVER DO IT. I asked Forest how long it took for him to come to terms with the notion that his parents actually DO, DO IT? He says it is only the last couple of years he has accepted it. Unfortunately, Danny was on the computer at the time and missed the whole thing and the discussion will have to be continued.

Anyway, I have to run. What I would really, really like is an invitation from you to spend the night in Calgary on Thursday night. If that doesn't work, I will phone my ex-stepdaughter and ask to stay with her.

Let me know if this suits you and if your heart is up to snuff.

Irene

Sent: October 31, 2006 10:10 P.M.
Subject: Irene's P.S.

I emailed Rosie as well and told her we were seeing each other, but she couldn't remember you. If you think she was wild..........she was always envious of me because I was single so long. I always did what I wanted, when I wanted and how I wanted. I was still very responsible and kind to the people I encountered and it was most often me who was let down.

My theory is you cannot live life full circle unless you experience all aspects of human existence and unfortunately for most they can't accept this. Like I always said to my parents (and everyone else who would listen) to truly live a full and wonderful life, you must also experience the pain or you will never quite get there.....I never seemed to mind thorns.

Irene

Sent: November 1, 2006 4:42 P.M.
Subject: Re...PS.....Hi there

Hi Irene,

Got your emails (large print)....can you dig it?....and all the talk of orgasm and all that and my mind started to race....Whoa....and we haven't even got it quite right...yet....then I had to focus a lot because I've got some music to prep for CFCN today....FO-CUS...you know from about age 40, sex and intimacy came after music and now I have to focus on music again and I'm not even close to 29!!!!!

I started to see how I can spend Thursday and immediately all sorts of booking issues started to emerge, all it took was a few phone calls to screw it up for me. I have to gig on Thursday evening and then I have to remix the keyboards on Ian Tyson's cuts that I did on Monday night. I tried to postpone it for Sunday but I have to play in Banff at Running Bull's for a benefit on Sunday....one of those calls....so my only time is tomorrow evening after my gig.

I've got to get my carcass downtown to the Delta Bow Valley now for five to put in two "Happy" hours at the baby grand....will touch base later.

Cephus

Sent: November 2, 2006 8:13 P.M.
Subject: Re: re...PS...Hi There

I have to thank you once more and this time for the word Whoa! (Large print). It has brought me to a very important realization about who and what I am. I knew there was a very good reason why we connected. I believe there are always reasons why people connect in life, if we watch close enough.

This whole week has been about my children and another lesson I had to teach them before they leave home. I mentioned to you before, I am not the type of person to keep secrets and I have never done so with my parents, my children or others I come in contact with. I try very hard to communicate my true feelings and try to dig out of others the same.

This is probably why in my life I have been blessed with such wonderful relationships with children and parents and I find most people sticking to me like glue, except of course, the ex. Sometimes people seem to be drawn to me as if they are trying to take some of my passion for life, which is something most lack.

I had coffee with an acquaintance last week and her reaction was exactly that. She was almost begging me to spend more time with her. Later, I had a call from this young girl I had met at Running Bull's the night we reconnected and she was doing the same. She wanted desperately for us to get together in Banff, to talk.

One of the last lessons I have to teach my children before they leave me is a lesson of PASSION and what it really means. Very little of it has to do with what goes on between the sheets. I have tried to live my whole life and all aspects of it, with a sometimes overwhelming passion. I have a great passion for my work, for business, for raising children, for having great parents, for travel, for play, for real estate, for friends and for having sex....passion for everything. I think I made a big mistake reading Gibran when I was younger.

So please don't tell me Whoa! You can say NO, but not Whoa! It is just not in my vocabulary.

Irene

Sent: November 2, 2006 8:25 P.M.
Subject: Hi there

Hi Irene,

Good morning……..sitting here at a computer at CFCN trying to squeeze a 30 second commercial……when your email arrived on my instant messenger. I thought you should know that……WHOA…. was for me and my mind and not for you. I was actually experimenting with the big print….OK.

Talk to you later…..

Cephus

Chapter 10

On his next visit, the story Cephus told me won my heart. He told me about how he instantly was attracted to me, that first night at Benny's. I was still married and everyone in the band knew it and yet he felt compelled to meet me. By the end of their first set, both Chuck and Greg knew Cephus was smitten with me. They all knew Cephus was not easily taken anymore with women.. Before the evening ended, the boys had given me the nickname, "Thou shalt not covet". When we booked an evening for the restaurant, Chuck would tell Cephus, "Thou shalt not covet," will be here tonight.

I thought the nickname was cute, but it did strike a chord with me. Quite possibly, I still felt married and no one would ever covet me. The divorce was not final and, in fact, the settlement by now had almost totally stalled.

Cephus continued with his story asking if I had noticed how each time John and I had arrived at the restaurant, that he would say to John, "Here comes the luckiest man in the Valley". He questioned me if I had not known what he meant by this. My response was that while I was married I had chosen to ignore advances and I hadn't noticed. Cephus ended his stories that evening, by telling me that he had waited two years for me. It was the first time in my life someone had waited for me.

Sent: November 3, 2006 11:26 A.M.
Subject: DMF tonight

Okay, I give up! If I don't get to touch your skin tonight, I will just up and die on you!

Irene

Sent: November 3, 2006 1:53 P.M.
Subject: DMF tonight

Hi Irene,

Please don't die on me. Now that's a loaded question....considering the very last time we were close.........mmm..........and you were on "me"......you certainly weren't dying.....as I pleasantly remember. Yes, I will be in DMF tonight and my skin + has been in anticipation of you for awhile too.............

Talk to you later

Cephus

Chapter 11

Sent: November 7, 2006 8:27 A.M.
Subject: Good morning Cephus

I had such a great day at work yesterday and a super night's sleep. It appears my body is getting somewhat back to normal....I think. I was up with the birds at 6:00 and am ready for the day.

I finally got the numbers together for my accountant and, hopefully, he will be able to get John and me closer to finalizing the divorce settlement. I can only hope, in the end, it won't cost me over half a million to end what he started.

I am taking my mother into the hospital today for her exploratory surgery. She is mentally prepared to do what it takes, which is good, because she will need the strength. I told them that we have had such a good relationship all these years and it was much like a marriage and we would continue to stick together and get through this, like my father's heart attack a year earlier. She felt a great deal better.

It seems my parents are quite content with this new relationship of mine. I think they know I function better when I have love in my life; otherwise I get too carried away with work and leave no time for myself. Everyone at work, on the other hand, keeps telling me if I don't slow down and take time for myself I will burn out. What they don't realize is that I only have one speed while working. Only on vacation do I understand slow.........and sometimes in bed while making love.

Which brings me right back to you again? When do you start playing in Banff on Thursdays? It would be nice to have you around more often. I had a look at your astrology sign, Taurus, and love on the internet. It said Taurus should be careful not to treat their lovers like trinkets or trophies they put on a shelf and occasionally dust. It goes on to say that if you treat them like this, they may slip through your fingers and be gone. I've printed it out and will show it to you later, as there is more. I still find this information quite interesting and I am sure we will find some truth to it before the day is done.

Regardless, I am not afraid. I have made it through twenty-four hours now and I can handle the next twenty-four........I hope. Tonight may be difficult though, as I have a friend with a girlfriend coming out from Calgary to stay the night. We are supposed to go out to the Bearin for drinks this evening and will wind up no doubt with me playing my Motown CD again… "Jimmy, Jimmy Mack, when are you Coming Back?"

Have a great day! It is now 8:50 and you are so much on my mind that I need a release of this excess energy you give to me. I have a staff meeting in half an hour…nice of you to join us at this meeting because you really are there in my head and elsewhere.

Irene

Sent: November 7, 2006 3:17 P.M.
Subject: 24 Hours NOT!

Okay….I tried but it didn't work…I had to come home at 3:00 o'clock and I think it is going to be a very long night!

You could just call me and say "hello" and possibly give me one of your laughs that I love so much. This would definitely make me feel better.

Good night and hope you have a great evening!

Irene

Sent: November 8, 2006 8:11 A.M.
Subject: Good morning

Hi Irene,

Good morning……I've been trying to send you this email and every time I hit send, my mailbox backs up and erases my message but I'll try again.

Cephus

Sent: November 8, 2006 8:32 A.M.
Subject: Finally.....

Hi there again Irene,

Gee, it finally worked...Yeah...When I was in my zone I sent you a couple of emails and couldn't get them sent and now the ideas and thoughts have sort of lost the spontaneity that they would have had and now it's just a note.

Needless to say...last weekend was beautiful...glad you could put in some work too and get positive responses from your clients and superiors too.

The Banff deal at Buffalo's doesn't start until next Thursday I think, but I'll keep you posted on that. Hope you didn't get too drinking....or too sexy, with your friends from Calgary, at the Bearin. We old musicians have seen a lot of episodes involving booze and sex... the booze cancels everything sexy....too many tales.

Thinking of you...that way too...got to run to Global T.V...will touch base later.

Cephus

Sent: November 8, 2006 9:51 A.M.
Subject: Thank you for hello and laugh

Thanks for the call this evening. I really needed that and my apologies for not picking up the phone the first time you called, but I couldn't. Yesterday turned out to be too horrible! It started out great and then by mid afternoon all the good feelings disappeared. I sent a three page email to John in response to his last three emails from yesterday alone and part of our negotiations. Unfortunately, it looks like we are right back to square one and he is sticking to his original expectations, which are, to say the least, outrageous.

The girls from Calgary cancelled, so I didn't go anywhere. All I did was have a battle with John over the internet and then I proceeded to have a battle with the children. It did not turn out well. Some days I just get tired of being used.

I have to take my mother to see the doctor at 2:00 o'clock and other than that, I am hiding today from the world. I am now going back to bed.

I did the laundry yesterday and went to change the sheets, but couldn't. I could still smell the sweet aroma of the weekend and decided to enjoy it a couple of days longer. Sometimes, it is important to enjoy the simple things in life.

Irene

Sent: November 10, 2006 7:58 A.M.
Subject: Poems

Good morning Cephus! I hope you slept well. The poems I wanted you to check out were by Dorothy Parker. The two that stand out in my mind right now, are, "On Cheating the Fiddler" and "The Whistling Girl". I have read most of them so many times now, I may have grown tired of them or maybe I just need to set the book aside again for a couple of years. I think what I would really like at this point, is an actual date with you. I mean some time together during the day or earlier in the evening for a few hours. Remember that song "After Midnight"? Well, I would like to see you sometime before midnight or do you never have time for this?

Last night I got this wonderful feeling, thinking it would be nice to watch a movie together or maybe even go to the hot pool in Banff. We could go to dinner somewhere or sit in some corner in a nice quiet place to talk and hold hands. What do you think? Would that be asking too much? I hope you don't plan to keep me only as your "After Midnight" girl.

I will really miss you tonight, if you don't have time. Hooked on You.....

Irene

Chapter 12

The relationship was turning out not to be what I had expected. We never saw each other until after midnight when he finished playing. I expected what every woman expects and that was a call to invite me out to dinner, the theatre, or better still, to hear him play somewhere in the city and then to go home with him afterwards. The invitations never came and we continued in the same way.

Joanna, my closest friend, began to question my judgement of Cephus. She wondered how I could be satisfied dating a man who never asked me out anywhere. Other girlfriends, not as close, such as Lily, Cynthia, Alycia and Diane, settled for giving me strange looks when I discussed Cephus, but they didn't say anything. They looked at me as if to say our love was only a figment of my imagination. I was, after all, a good storyteller.

I felt that I should let him lead with the relationship and see how it progressed. If I felt it didn't appear to be working, then I basically had three choices. The first, of course, would be to walk away and say nothing; the second would be to try to take charge of the situation and effectively meet halfway with changes that needed to be made; or the final option would be to say nothing and accept things as they were. For the time being I chose the latter.

Cephus was not one to take very many days without a gig and he was more fanatic about his work, or should I say "play" as he called it, than even I. I was accustomed to listening to him until 3:00 or 4:00 A.M. on the evenings of his visits. After very enjoyable sex, we would go to sleep and stay in bed until noon the next day. In the mornings he would continue with all of his stories.

Many of these were of his everyday life in Chateaubelair, at a time when there still wasn't any electricity. The first time Cephus went home, after visiting his father in the city, he told his friends how they actually had street lights. They mocked him and thought he made it up. Another story told about the early morning ritual of jumping into the ocean to bathe before school, after which they would grab a piece of arrowroot from the fields to brush their teeth. Cephus's mother owned one of the grocery stores and he did have a real toothbrush at home. He wanted to be like the rest and even though he already brushed with the real thing earlier, he brushed again with the arrowroot and his friends.

I never tired of his stories and the most amazing thing for me was how enjoyable sex was and, at sixty-three, it seemed he could also never get enough. Only once before had I experienced such an insatiable lust for another. We were like the proverbial rabbits doing it five or six times by midmorning. I thought this was amazing stamina for a man of his age.

Sent: November 12, 2006 7:21 P.M.
Subject: Funeral Services

This morning I was glued to the television from 10:55 onward, in hopes of seeing your son, Jordon, sing the national anthem for the Grey Cup, but it never came on. It appears they just skipped right over the anthem and went right into the game. Why would they do that? This would never happen in American football!

Funeral services for my co-worker and her husband went fairly well. The Radisson Hotel was packed with family, co-workers and friends. The family seemed to cope rather well, but then they had had a month to begin to deal with the grief. It was so sad to see the two children. The daughter brought this giant teddy bear for company. I managed through it all right, thanks to Joanna on one side and Jessica and her boyfriend on the other. The emotion has left me drained and I am ready for bed as soon as I finish saying goodnight to you.

I will write more in another email.

Irene

Sent: November 12, 2006 7:46 P.M.
Subject: Goodnight

There was still so much I wanted to say to you this morning, but there wasn't enough time. Usually when that happens, I just continue to have the conversation with myself, which is what I did. Now comes the tricky part of trying to remember it all, which probably won't happen, considering the fact that I am exhausted. I just can't find the words tonight. I will try again tomorrow.

Pleasant dreams
Irene

Sent: November 13, 2006 9:23 A.M.
Subject: Good Morning

Hi Irene,

Yeah, I hear that the National Anthem wasn't shown on television. I guess Canucks aren't as patriotic as Yanks, who sing their anthem anytime more than seven of them are gathered together, even for a crab race. Jordon called me just before they sang, as I was pulling into the parking lot of the church to play. I made it on time and they were pleased.

Sounds like the memorial service went off well. I suppose after a month the acceptance has replaced the grief and the loss, but you sounded like you were drained afterward.

Hope your all day course today keeps you alert. Knock them dead.

Will touch base later
Cephus

Part Three
Feast or Famine

Chapter 13

Sent: November 13, 2006 6:33 P.M.
Subject: Feast or Famine

Virgo the worrier:

When you left yesterday I had this thought; maybe you think of me as some sex fiend. I didn't start to worry necessarily, but I did start to ask myself if it were true. Definitely not, was the answer!

My whole life flashed before my eyes as I revisited all those years of work and travel and the relationships that came between. Many of the early years I found myself preoccupied with notions of becoming the second Mother Teresa, even though I already had a couple of transgressions.

In case you were wondering I have never had sex on:

Trinidadian soil – ignored the potentials

African soil – turned down all prospects in three countries

Samoan soil – almost but he couldn't perform

Australian soil – gave the guy from Samoa a second chance and still nothing happened

New Zealand soil – nothing

Japanese soil – (both trips) first trip was still with thoughts of Mother T and the only thing I lost were locks of my hair that I braided and gave to an American soldier there

British soil – (both trips) ignored all advances

French soil – (all trips) I think the one was gay – nothing

German soil – (all trips) my first kiss and nothing more

American soil – (all trips) nothing even on one trip there with a boyfriend and his parents and 200 pound sister....I slept with the sister

I don't think you can call that promiscuous, although I didn't name all the countries. Don't forget many of those trips were for months at a time. While at home I had longer term relationships, generally one to two years. You see it tended to be feast or famine with me. Travel to other countries not mentioned, is when I generally feasted, but it certainly wasn't often. Back home, if I were in a relationship, I could feast and, if not, I would starve myself.

It wasn't until I was approaching thirty all hell broke loose with my need to give birth. I call them my five years of hell. I had a multitude of male friends, none of which I saw in the day as I was too busy working. They seemed to end as quickly as they began and the next thing I knew, I decided it was time to read the Bible, cover to cover. Then came "you know who" and marriage at thirty-four and two children in rapid succession afterward.

On Saturday night you brought another tear to my eye, because of the overwhelming power you seem to possess over my body and mind. I say my mind, because I know all those married years, I never had a tear drop for that reason. I always managed to maintain control of my emotions and I think over this past weekend, I came to realize something very important. I must admit there is a possibility of actually having married him only to have children. Now, that would be sad. Maybe he realized it all along and I just didn't see it.

Only twice in my life, have I allowed someone to have so much control over me—the two relationships just prior to my marriage. With all the others, I remained guarded. At the moment, I find this very strange behaviour, on my part, as I still don't know who you really are; but I am bound and determined to enjoy this feast. There are still some questions in my mind and maybe you can answer them for me.

The first and most important question has to do with the possibility of my coming into the city this week. I mentioned it on the weekend when you were here and I half expected a response like "which day" or "Thursday would work for me". Your silence left me thinking one of five different possible scenarios:

1. He really is married.
2. He lives with his daughter and family.
3. He doesn't want anyone to know he is seeing you.
4. He doesn't want to see you on his turf.
5. His place is such a mess it would take him a month to clean it first.

I think that is enough rambling for now. I actually made dinner for everyone, including the children's friends and it is ready now. Tonight I want you to go to bed with just one thought in your mind.............a chair and a little lap dance.

Irene

Chapter 14

I enjoyed opening up and revealing all of my inner most thoughts to Cephus. My emails began to serve as a self analysis which I preferred over seeking professional help. I denied I needed any help after the demise of my marriage because I was happy. My ex was always so quick to recommend his rebuilding groups and the like. Regardless, I did find it somewhat therapeutic and I began writing even more. The increasing frequency of the emails could have resulted because of the rare opportunities to speak when we were together.

Sent: November 16, 2006 7:31 A.M.
Subject: Happy Thursday from Canmore

I found myself up with the birds again on this fine Thursday morning! I have to get into the office early today, after spending the last couple of days in the city. Now I am really behind, but I did get quite a bit done in Calgary. I half expected a note from you on my return, but no doubt you are back to checking your emails once a week or maybe you didn't quite know how to respond to my last email. Actually no response is fine as most of this will hopefully be in book form some day.....Harlequin Romance.

As much as I hate the city, it does have some advantages. I think I might like to learn Salsa dancing. You know what they say. It is never too late and it is definitely something every woman my age needs, that and a personal trainer. Besides, it might get me back into shape. I have signed Julianna and me up again for the gym and she is happy. Last winter we were going about three times a week, until we went to Mexico and then we sort of fizzled out.

I hope your week has gone well and just think it is Thursday. Remember the Parker poem..."the morrow touched our eyes; and found us walking firm above the ground"...we are still alive.

I have to get into the shower, before the line up starts. I will talk to you later.

Irene

Chapter 15

That weekend his discussions centered on the repackaging of women after they go through a divorce and their attempts at giving up the domestic side of themselves. Cephus never appeared to be judgmental with these stories and the depth of them I found fascinating.

In the clubs, Cephus had watched women for years. They would come in during their 20s, all decked out in their finest and sexiest clothes in hopes of meeting Mr. Right. The next thing he knew, he would not see them again for six or seven years. He assumed they had gone off to have their 1.2 children. Then, suddenly one night, there they were again, and alone. They had repackaged themselves with hair color and makeup in order to conceal their years of wisdom, domesticity and nurturing of children. The big question he had for me this weekend was: how much could a man truly trust a woman who would camouflage her true self with hair color and makeup? If he spotted from behind real grey hair in a woman, he was more curious about what the woman looked like. He continued telling me that while growing up in Chateaubelair, the men were always most attracted to the women with the hairy legs and armpits on the beach.. This was a sign of puberty and that women were ready for sex.

Chapter 16

Sent: November 20, 2006 3:11 P.M.
Subject: Buffalo's/Banff

Hi

I can't believe I was actually late for work this morning, for the first time. I woke up at 7:00 and then fell asleep again until 8:40, then the mad dash out the door. I must have been having more of those sweet dreams of you. I took Danny to the doctor yesterday, as his neck glands are still very swollen and he couldn't talk or eat. They will let us know what it is, in the next couple of days. He had strep last month and it could be back. I hope it isn't mumps.

I had a call from Lily and Peter from Banff and they noticed you were scheduled to play Buffalo's on Thursday. They wanted to know if I would join them to come hear you play. Let me know if you don't mind my attending as I don't want people to think I am some sort of groupie, following you around the various venues in the valley.

On another note, my mother's birthday went well and I could not believe the whole crew of them waited until 2:00 o'clock for me to join them for lunch. I went over there as soon as you left and there they were, waiting patiently. They knew I was making breakfast for us and were willing to wait. They do know what is important in life…love and the making of it is always supposed to come first. I am glad we all think alike and everyone was happy.

They are so supportive of me and what I do. They are all happy "you know who" is not a part of my life anymore. It is amazing what we live with and never quite see it for what it is. Especially for me, as I do have a tendency of living in my own special little world. I find most everything good and there are always GOOD reasons why we are given difficult situations to deal with in life. I look at them as boulders set in our path and tend to ultimately thank God for them. They give us the challenge to find a way under, over or around them and ultimately educate and inspire us. I keep thinking of the rose I enjoy so much. I cannot expect it comes without the thorn.

It was the first time my brother and his wife found out that I was seeing someone. I think your idea of this being your average small town, complete with its rumour mill is incorrect. They were happy to hear that you were a kind and gentle soul with an even temperament. They are all of the opinion I had enough of someone shaking their finger in my face, in one of their many mood swings. They are thankful I survived those eighteen years and can now get on with my life and are hopeful my next selection is better than the last. I am certain it will be as the pressures of those childbearing years are now behind me. I can focus more on my own needs in life as Julianna and Danny get ready to leave my nest.

What are those needs? Right now it is quite apparent to me; I need someone that makes me feel special and I definitely need the kindness and the, oh so, gentle touch. I need to be caressed and what I have really missed all those married years is the KISS! This is something I didn't realize until you came along and now I know how starved I was in those years of supposed marital bliss. You said on the weekend that the most important thing to you in a relationship is the passion, which really struck me. I discovered yesterday this is something I should not have denied myself. As a result I have done a great injustice to not only me, but to John as well.

In my first year of marriage was when I discovered I had possibly made a mistake and I should have ended it then and yet I chose to enter into this huge "learning curve". The marriage vows actually meant a great deal to me and I took them seriously.

Getting back to the passion and a much happier thought for me and then I need to end it on that note. I need to thank you for the wonderful weekend, first for the chair experience, which I would definitely do again; then the next evening with its oral stimulation which was phenomenal; however, I would like to end it differently next time; and finally, the wonderfully relaxing Sunday morning in bed with no rush other than the normal rushes between the sheets with you. Now I am all worked up again, but I promise I will save it for you.

Irene

P.S. Good thing no one is standing over my shoulder reading this. I did have to minimize a few times though.

Sent: November 21, 2006 2:36 A.M.
Subject: Hi there…Good morning

Hi Irene,

First of all I must tell you that during my drive back to Calgary on Sunday, it occurred to me that something happened to us on Saturday night and Sunday morning to make it sort of special. I don't know what it was but I'll try to find it again though. It was delightful and I thank you.

Of course you can come to Buffalo's with your friends. If it does not affect your business status in the Valley, what do you care what people think? Chuck and Greg know that we have been seeing each other.

Glad to hear that your mother's birthday went well. Hope you took that bright smile that I left you with at the door, with you to the gathering. Twas nice and I will give you a shout later on. Have a great day.

Cephus

Something did happen that weekend between us. I had now fallen in love with this man. I never before met someone who tried so hard to understand women and I was happy he was willing to get to know me. I was no longer just infatuated, but I had literally been swept off my feet by this secret admirer of mine.

Part Four
The First "I LOVE YOU"

Chapter 17

Sent: November 21, 2006 1:06 P.M.
Subject: The Repackaging of Irene

My mother's surgery went well this morning, but she sure was in a foul mood. She didn't sleep all night and wasn't able to smoke all day yesterday, which really finished her off emotionally. We have left her to sleep for a couple of hours and then we will go back to see her. Her spirit should be back by then.

Now I remember what I started to think about on the weekend when you mentioned the word "repackaging". Julianna gave me a huge gift on Sunday night when she came home from the movies with her friends. The gift she gave was herself and keeping me in touch with her thoughts. What she could have done was tune me out like most teenagers do to their parents and she couldn't. Thank God for that!

She said she was very upset with me when she stormed out yesterday. At first, I thought it was because of the fact that I had smoked in the house and after prying it from her, I found out that it had nothing to do with that. My second guess was that it had something to do with you and it wasn't that either.

It turns out Julianna and Danny, are both upset with me because of the second subject you mentioned over the weekend, my domesticity. I don't cook anymore! How natural for children to want what we all find comforting, which is to be at home with a home cooked meal. When I suggested they learn how to cook for themselves, Julianna suggested she would have the rest of her life to learn how to cook and for the little time she had left under my roof she thinks that I should continue to do the cooking.

When John left us, all domesticity was quickly sacrificed for a career and g enough earnings to pay the mortgages on the four properties. Unfortunately I had to put the children, my parents and dinner on the back burner.

Besides the cooking, Julianna misses our nightly talks and just spending quality time together. This is something I really miss as well. There wasn't a day went by when we didn't all spend time, individually and together, talking about anything they wanted to discuss. The subjects ranged from religion, politics, music, finances, homework , sex and anything in between.

I have discovered this repackaging of me has cost us all a great deal of emotions. We have all had to undergo these changes forced on us by John. My children really miss having a full-time "domesticated" mother around and I miss their company. I waited so long to have children; age thirty-six with Julianna and thirty-seven with Danny and I loved being their mother and was thankful for having them. I have always been proud of them and I have enjoyed watching them grow through all their stages. I would hate to think I would miss these last couple of years with them. Lately, all they have is a career person for a mother and they really don't know who I have become. Needless to say, I prepared a nice meal last night so I haven't totally forgotten my way around in the kitchen.

Well I had better get back to work for awhile and then back to my mother as I have another date with my kitchen this evening. The nice thing about that is I can't smell the smoke anymore in the house from when I cheat and smoke indoors over the weekend when you are here.

Who knows? I may even cook for you someday. I think something like a curried mango chicken would be nice. You know what they say is the only way to a man's heart is through his stomach. Right now it is where I would like to be if there is room…I mean in your heart and not your stomach.

Irene

P.S. Good morning starts at 2:30 A.M. for you?

Sent: November 22, 2006 10:27 A.M.
Subject: No Room?

Well you don't need to reply so quickly to my questions. All I asked was if you had a LITTLE ROOM and not a lot. After all, I have saved a little spot for you. How else could I possibly get into you any other way? There is that silly word again, INTO. I think I am a sick woman! It seems like most of the day this is all I want to think about lately, but you must admit the thoughts are pleasant ones. It must be an obsessive compulsive disorder. I'll have it checked.

I wound up taking Danny into emergency last night around midnight. He woke up with such a bad earache. It turns out it is only viral. He has a bad cold with a minor ear infection. I always worry when he gets sick as he was born so premature. He arrived three and one half months early, weighing only 1.6 pounds and he spent the first three months of his life in the neonatal intensive care unit at the Foothills.

We have been lucky with his health so far as most of these children have ongoing health issues. I still worry though that one day something will show up as a result of his premature birth. Anyway, we finally got to bed around 1:30 A.M. and I will have to work late in order to get caught up.

Julianna and I went to see my mom twice last night and she is finally recovering from the mastectomy. At first they couldn't get the bleeding to stop and thought they would have to operate again and then finally it slowed down. She should be able to come home soon. My poor father is just so lost without her. I can't imagine what he would do if she were gone as he seems to live for her most days.

I have to go sell a house now. It has been quiet the last week. Apparently, it gets this way just before Christmas and not many want to move this time of year. I'll have to see what I can shake loose. The elderly woman in the room with my mother fell down a flight of fifteen stairs. Maybe she needs to move to a single level home.

"Later" seems to be a favourite word of yours.

Irene

Sent: November 23, 2006 8:33 A.M.
Subject: More on Later

Good morning Cephus

It is snowing a fair bit this morning and the roads are not the best today. Please remember one of your favourite words….later. Remember it is better to arrive "later" than not at all. Drive carefully tonight in your mad dash from playing the Delta in Calgary to playing Buffalo's in Banff. I want to see you here…..later.

Irene

Chapter 18

Cephus began to enjoy all this mail that he was receiving and it almost became a daily routine for me. He became dependant on hearing from me and when I missed a day he would phone in a panic and he wanted to know if something was wrong. He found his fingers took too long to find the right keys and he didn't write very often, but he preferred to call and even that seemed to be fairly infrequent.

If I didn't write as often as I did, we seemed to lose touch with each other and I was afraid we would drift apart. Relationships are difficult enough without having all these miles that separated us and I was beginning to feel the distance. I wanted to see more of him, which at the time was generally twice a week.

That Saturday was my belated birthday gathering at Benny's. I looked forward to this evening, but was nervous. It would be the first time since the relationship began that I had danced in front of him, while he was playing.. Unfortunately, it turned out rather awkward for both Cephus and me. The tequila that Chuck and the rest kept bringing didn't help.

At the end of the evening I told everyone to leave without me and I would go home once Cephus finished packing up his gear. While I was waiting for him, I moved to the bar to speak to Fritz, rather than sit alone. Fritz owned an Inn in Canmore and we had known each other for almost twenty years. I was not even remotely attracted to this man and I certainly wasn't that night either. He wore a red and black hunting jacket which I found appalling.

On the way home I asked Cephus if he wanted to park somewhere and make love but he was agitated. Back in Canmore, he noticed he forgot his glasses at Benny's and he blamed me and was even more annoyed. We had our first fight. Cephus said I acted like the other drunken women whom he had seen in bars all those years. I was puzzled why he blamed me for leaving his glasses behind. My opinion was that he was jealous when I had danced with other men in our group and when I had spent time talking to Fritz.

I found out he had one time taken a woman he loved to one of his gigs. She was dancing with another man and she actually left with him. Through his forty years as a full time musician, he knew better than most; he knew what men and women were capable of when they were out drinking and looking for a good time. He had seen all these women out looking for Mr. Right, as he calls it. He was tired of the countless times women, who after too many drinks, had tried to pick up the piano player at the end of the night and who could blame him.

He had not lived the life of a Puritan by any means and had taken countless women up on their offers from coast to coast and sea to sea. In St.Vincent, he fell in love with a high school sweetheart. While playing in Barbados, Antigua and all those other islands, he was, as my father described, "one of those musicians with a woman in every port". This story and those of others, made me wonder why it seemed fine for the rest of the world to be wild and free and I should stick to my Bible. Maybe it was the MT on my forehead.

Cephus told me about a woman from Winnipeg whom he had met in Antigua. Six months later, he flew to Toronto from there to do a weekend gig. He had the evening off when they first arrived and decided to hop on a bus and surprise this woman with a visit. About four hours later he asked the driver how much further was this place. When he found out it was a twelve hour drive, he hopped off and got onto the next bus heading in the opposite direction. She never found out that he was even in the country. She must have been very good to him.

He left that Sunday telling me he was not my "toy boy" and I should look in the mirror to find my answers. I was miserable and hung over and wasn't sure if I wanted to see him again.

Chapter 19

Sent: November 28, 2006 9:52 A.M.
Subject: Hi There

Hi Irene,

How are you doing? I know that tequila doesn't have much of a hangover potential so I hope you are ok and was able to work reasonably on Sunday afternoon. I tried to do that myself but you kept popping into my head over and over again....Hmmmmm

Anyway, I haven't heard from you by email and I miss your contact already and I want to hear from you. I hope you aren't cold on me as the weather is. That is after Saturday night's?#%@.

Did you ever find out what happened to Joanna and why she didn't show up for your party? I'd like to know because she is your best friend and you guys are pretty deep.

Hope your mom is recovering nicely. She has a great caretaker.... you.

You are on my mind....lots.

Luv
Cephus

This was the first time that Cephus had used the word "Luv" to sign off and I was thrilled to see the word in print. I never expected to hear from him again. The one thing I began to notice was when I stopped writing, then he would miraculously find the keys to type or find the time to phone more often. I asked myself the question: could I stop writing and play hard to get? Obviously, it was something I was not good at.

Sent: November 28, 2006 5:14 P.M.

Subject: Hello

When you called the first time this morning, I was in the regular Tuesday morning staff meeting and we are not allowed to have our phones on. The second time you called I was in a co-worker's car doing the regular Tuesday morning realtors' open house tour and I had my phone in my bag and still turned off.

You must be busy yourself because I left you a message three minutes after your last call and I got your voice mail. I took my mother back into the hospital for her follow up appointment and everything seems to be healing fairly well. Apparently, the cancerous node was very small and it doesn't appear to have spread.

As for the rest, I am certainly not cold on you like this weather. On the contrary, I am hot as usual. I am digging into my Christmas baking and doing cookies for this Friday and "Light up Canmore". I will be keeping the office open late and will serve hot chocolate and the cookies. So I am busy in the kitchen, at work and looking in the mirror as you suggested on the weekend. As a matter of fact, I have been absolutely miserable since you left on Sunday. I have been carrying a tissue around just in case I need it. I have been trying to figure out what happened to us on Saturday night.

Since Sunday I have received emails from my friends at the club on Saturday and they all say they had a great time. I know I had more than enough tequila that night and I thought I had better check with some of them to see if they thought I did something that could have gotten you so upset with me. The general consensus is that they believe I behaved very well and did nothing wrong.

I would like to add my thoughts on the evening. I went there wanting you to feel like the "luckiest guy in the Valley" for a change, instead of John. I know you were working, but I thought you could enjoy our being there together under the same roof. Maybe it was the memory of your old girlfriend and nothing more. I can assure you of one thing, when I am with someone, and regardless of the number of tequilas consumed, I could never look at another man much less do something worse.

For most of the evening on Saturday, all I could think was how

64

nice it would be to have an evening like that with you sitting beside me, instead of up on stage. How nice it would be to have your arm around me and to dance with you. The parameters, you seem to have set for this relationship, however, do not seem to allow for that. I really do feel like "your after midnight girl" and maybe that is part of our problem.

I think the simple truth is that I wanted to be with you and you wanted to be with me and yet we both knew we were going to have to wait until......later. For the time being, I won't be going any-where you are playing as I think it is too hard on both of us.

I need to phone for a doctor's appointment to see if she can ex-plain what this burning sensation is in my chest.

Irene

P.S. I think I like the "Luv" better than the "Later". I love you too. And I forgot to thank you for the music on Saturday night. It took so much effort on your part to put it all together. It did not go unnoticed and was much appreciated!

Sent: November 29, 2006 10:30 A. M.
Subject: Good Morning Larry

It seems like you got your fix yesterday with my email and now I can wait for a reply until much later. Well, you were partly right yesterday about the weather. I was going to keep writing, but was not going to hit send anymore and instead keep it for myself. I keep doing this maximum exposure thing which I can't change about my personality. It leaves me totally vulnerable and exposed. I suppose it is one way of knowing we are truly alive and breathing.

Anyway, I need to ask you a couple of questions before I decide whether or not to stop hitting the send button. At the staff meet-ing yesterday they wanted a head count for the December 15th staff Christmas party. Will you be able to make it or not? The second question is a big one and maybe you should take some time to think about it before giving me your answer. John is taking the kids to Vancouver for Christmas, December 26th to January 3rd. What do you plan on doing with me that week?

Here are some suggestions:

1. We could go to Mexico for the week. Just the two of us.

2. I could stay with you in Calgary that week and actually cook for you.

3. Do nothing with me that week other than the usual after midnight thing.

Joanna wants me to go to Mexico with her that week and she wants us to book the flights. Let me know sometime soon.

Luv
Irene

Sent: November 30, 2006 1:54 P.M.

Subject: A Story from Me to You

I need to tell you a story now about that first night we reconnected at Running Bull's. You keep telling me it was you who waited these three years and you were first attracted to me. I have been thinking about this since the first time those sweet words rang in my ears.

When I first saw you that night I felt so drawn to you. That is why I risked getting my mother so upset with me when I did not go home with them. I needed and wanted to be with you at any price. I have come to the conclusion I too must have been attracted to you all along and because I was married at the time, I chose to ignore all the warning signs. The weeks following that first night, I remember feeling as if I had discovered something I thought I would never find again in my lifetime. I told you, that only once before have I loved a man as deeply or as passionately the way I love you.

I am simple crazy about you! It seems like this is all I want to think about these days. My feelings for you frighten me because I can't explain them or justify them as I still don't know you all that well. All I know is that they are quite overwhelming at times.

The one thing I do know for certain is you are not my "toy boy" and it is not only about the sex. Remember, I have also had plenty of that in my day. I have always known how fussy I am with men and I trust my intuition and have to go with that. All I know right now is I want to be with you and how this story will end, I don't think either of us knows.

The End or the Beginning?
Irene

Part Five
The First Date

Chapter 20

Sent: December 1, 2006 11:19 A.M.
Subject: On Exposing One's self

I spent this whole week with so many highs and lows and yet it ultimately turned out to be a truly inspirational one for me, thanks to Tolstoy's "Confession". I started reading the book in Mexico, the previous Christmas, when I was there with Joanna and all the kids. I put the book away with the bookmark on page 99. When I picked it up again, there it was, the essence of the work, staring me in the face.

All those months of not looking at the book, I wondered what was going through his mind and I couldn't understand his purpose for writing it in the first place. Could he have struggled so long and hard with this simple question of the true meaning of life and the spiritual being of mankind?

About halfway through the book he finally discovers we do not appear on earth without meaning or motive. Something I have always felt so strongly about. I believe everything we do in life and all the people we meet are for a purpose. They are all one more piece of this giant puzzle, which in the end makes us whole and complete. I once wrote the definition of who I am; a small part of everyone I ever met before. I have taken something from everyone and only hope I was able to take only the good from those I have met.

Tolstoy looks at birds and notices they only live to fly, eat and to build their nests. He sees the simplicity of their lives as possibly the key to a happy existence. This was something both my parents taught me throughout my life and was something I did understand, although I found it difficult at times to incorporate into my everyday life and especially in those years of owning the store. You also understand this well, but unlike me, you find it an easy principle to follow. This is another one of those characteristics of yours I love so much.

Tolstoy sees the normal sufferings of mankind as making them whole and bringing them closer to God and to the light. Once we are closer to God, we cannot help, but find happiness. To fully enjoy the rose, one must also accept the thorns.

When I read Tolstoy's suggestion that we forget the ways of the flesh, I started to cry, thinking my day yesterday with you was, in Tolstoy's interpretation, only "enjoyment of the flesh" and was somehow evil. How could he possibly be more wrong?

The whole day, after you left, I found my body was filled with thousands of electrical bolts rushing through it, anytime I would think of you. Contrary to what Tolstoy thinks, I believe this love, along with the currents, was sent to me by God and they were good and not evil, as he suggests. Human sexuality was, and is, a gift from God and as natural and simple as a bird building a nest. We would all do well to stop thinking of it as some wicked pass time and we will be damned for life if we find ourselves truly enjoying it.

Every once in awhile, I catch myself with feelings of guilt for enjoying myself so immensely with my own thoughts and this is what has been happening to me all week. The other side of this is, I can also languish in such agony over things and I enjoy it as well. I know how refreshing it feels when it is over. Experiencing the unpleasant heightens the enjoyment of the pleasant.

Once again continuing with Tolstoy, has taught me never to give up and I was happy that I had found those words. The next day I woke up free from the chains of guilt that haunted me this week and I found renewed energy in the many gifts of God.

It is important in life to totally envelop it and learn how to expose yourself. Remember the words about either standing for something or falling for everything. We waste so much precious time in our lives with fear of this exposure of our inner beings. What we don't realize is, through this maximum exposure, comes such happiness and freedom. In fact, I have always been of the opinion this is the only means by which we can achieve greatness in whatever we do in life.

Many people do not know how to embrace all of the human emotions given to them and, instead, they run from them, hide from them, deny them or just fear them altogether. Allowing ourselves the freedom to completely experience all forms of these emotions, and from the depths of one's being, can give us such power and energy. This overwhelming passion for life could ultimately relinquish us from all fear, including that of death.

I have tried very hard in my life to live this way. I was always an "all or nothing" type of person. I would prefer to go through life thinking that every happy as well as every sad song that was ever written, was written for me. Remember the Parker poem that says, "Better a heart abloom with sins than hearts gone yellow and dry". I think it is crucial to my happiness and fulfillment in life that I try to put my heart and soul into all things I undertake. Be it with my work, my play and yes, even with sex, it is important to try not to be just lukewarm about things in life. What an injustice for all, to settle for mere lukewarm, as Gibran suggested.

I think that is why I believe my life has been successful and I can honestly say I have very few regrets about all things past. This is also the reason I am not afraid to answer any questions about the things I do or have done, whether they be good or bad. Mistakes in life are the educators and should be treated as such and not with embarrassment, but as mere occurrences.

Most often, I believe I possess this energy or power and that is why some people seem to gravitate to me, thinking they can sap some of it for themselves and yet there are others who choose to run like hell, because they are afraid of it. I have watched the look on people's faces and I recognize when they are taking my energy for their own. Little do they know, unless they find theirs, mine will not last with them very long.

I think childbirth has softened this power, as have the years, and

I find fewer people frightened by it. They do not seem to feel as threatened. Could all this that I just wrote be the reason for this new relationship and for developing a clearer understanding of me, of whom and what I am? After all, you are the one who told me to look in the mirror this week. Well, I have been looking and I don't mind what I see.

The blank page is wonderful and much like new beginnings. I needed to get back to this subject of exposure again. It was difficult for me all these years, to find simpler words to describe this principle to Julianna and Danny. I have tried many different ways and yet, I still see them doing things half-heartedly, and this tells me that they haven't understood it fully yet.

What I find is most people tend to live their lives like this. They are quick to blame others for their failures, misery, lack of living and happiness. Instead of taking their lives into their own hands and making of it what they will, they give the power away so easily for others to control their destinies and their emotions.

Life is about choices and there are always loads of them, much like this blank page. We each get to choose what goes on the pages of our life. If we have maintained control of our emotions and hold no one to blame for these, each end will promise a new beginning to something even better. How happy we should be to find in place another piece of the puzzle to our lives..

I don't think Joanna understands this concept and I have spent the last year trying to explain it to her. I really think she believes if she falls off the horse, she will never ride again. She couldn't be more wrong. Just think of all the life she is missing, because of her fears of exposure. I think I should give Joanna my "one hundred and one ways to get over a guy "and maybe that would help her start her new beginning.

On the other hand, I think what makes me so different from others, is I use every ounce of my energy to move as quickly as possible on to the next thing. At work, everyone appears to be amazed at my enthusiasm in doing anything and everything and how I rarely say "no" when asked to do something. I have moved into this new career quickly and with purpose. The longer a person drags their heels, the longer life remains uncomfortable when change must occur. Don't get me wrong as I do know how to take life slowly as well. But like making love, it doesn't always have to be slow and easy; rather sometimes it can be fast and furious. It prevents us from getting bored with repetition.

Chapter 21

Sent: December 2, 2006 1:10 P.M.
Subject: Answer to Chest Pain

Hello Cephus

I have finally figured out what this burning sensation is in my chest. I don't think it is sympathy for my mother, nor do I believe it to be from the ab machine at the gym and I certainly don't think it is some cancer growing in me. It starts in my nipples and moves in both directions to under my armpits and it is not really an ache as such and, therefore, I believe you have a great deal to do with it.

Have a great day!

Irene

Sent: December 2, 2006 5:18 P.M.
Subject: Amusement

One of the many things my father taught me is to never look to others for one's happiness and in order to love others in life, one must first learn how to love one's self. A truer statement was never spoken. Whatever emotions you carry in your heart is what you will ultimately live, be it love, self doubt, hatred, fear and all the endless emotions humans can feel.

Over the last twenty-five years, I have managed to build for myself a wonderful little world in my mind where I spend a great deal of time. It has been a challenge to perfect this world and to rid it of the negative human emotions. I have not totally succeeded, but I do believe I am closer than most. One of the reasons I say this is because when something does not go according to my plan in life or appears to be out of my control, I quickly make a new plan that does make me happy and may bring success to my life in what I want to achieve.

More important is that I have gotten very good at being able to amuse myself with my own thoughts. I have become so adept at this self entertainment I can go on for hours and, in fact, I believe that is where I have spent the better part of the last eighteen years and thus managed to survive them, virtually unscathed and still with little regret.

Ultimate in this control of our own mind is the ability to create multiple orgasms without man or vibrator. Don't get me wrong, like the song...."Ain't nothing like the real thing baby".

Irene

Sent: December 4, 2006 11:39 A.M.

Subject: Staff Christmas

You forgot to tell me, when you called before, whether or not you would be able to make it to the staff Christmas party on the 15th. I thought there was a chance someone could fill in for you that night or maybe I hoped the two of them would be able to go it alone for either all or just half the night.

Anyway, the staff meeting is tomorrow morning and that is the deadline for the headcount so if I don't hear from you by then, I will tell them I will be a single. This could be another misfortune for you as I am planning on wearing the same thing I had on last Saturday at Benny's. Maybe this time you could get some enjoyment out of it. Otherwise I will go to plan B and wear what I had on at the Hyatt, which is definitely far less sexy. I was hoping, if you came, everyone from work would be able to meet my preoccupation!

Hope your day goes well and you are not too tired.

Irene

Chapter 22

The one thing that was beginning to bother me and was difficult to deal with, was the fact that I found myself asking all these questions that went unanswered, as if they didn't matter. The first time I asked about the Christmas party was on the 29th of November and it was now a week later and I still didn't know. I also had never received an answer about what he planned to do with me between Christmas and New Year's.

When someone asks a question of another, it is generally considered rude not to answer. I guess Cephus didn't see it this way. Maybe it is a cultural thing, like his birth right or something. This hurt me very much and I felt like my feelings didn't matter and I didn't deserve an answer.

Sent: December 5, 2006 11:35 A.M.
Subject: Hi

Hi Irene,

It was nice to hear from you, of course. Yeah, I don't think we talked about the party but that night, December 15, is a very important night at Benny's, so important that Chuck had to re-negotiate with Greg and me to prevent us from staying and playing at functions in Calgary that weekend. We did that last year so I'll just have to hook up with you afterwards at your soiree…later (chuckle)…this is the busy season.

Hope your band house deal was positive and your mother's surgery too…will contact you again soon.

Luv

CJ

Sent: December 5, 2006 12:29 P.M.
Subject: Coffee Wednesday

Thank you for getting back to me. I already told them this morning, they would have to wait until after Francois Restaurant to meet you. My mother is still in the hospital until later today. They only checked to see how deep this ran and will do the necessary surgery later this week. She has become so depressed the last few days. That's why she was upset with me. I didn't call her back quickly enough when I was coming home from Banff on Sunday.

Yesterday turned out to be a huge real estate day for me, in spite of how exhausted I was. Remember what I said before about understanding "No", but "Whoa" was not in my vocabulary. The same goes for real estate. My broker suggested the same this morning, saying I was doing way more than my share of floor duty. I haven't got a clue what he is talking about as I am doing much less at this point in my life than at any other.

To me it feels like I am operating only at half speed, possibly due to my age and current distraction. I told my parents when I began this new career, if I only do half of what I normally did and was capable of, I would be doing extremely well financially and they agreed.

Anyway, I need to get back to work. I almost forgot to ask you something, the reason I actually hit reply in the first place. I desperately need to come into Calgary either tomorrow or Thursday morning. I will only have a window of about a half hour. I thought we could meet somewhere for coffee. Phone me on my cell and let me know which day would be better for you.

Irene

Chapter 23

Sent: December 7, 2006 8:56 A.M.
Subject: WOW! OUR FIRST DATE

Finally we've had our first real date with coffee yesterday, in public and it wasn't even dark! It was short and hectic with the traffic, but wonderful all the same. It was nice to be able to get together in the daytime for a change. I promise I will never again call myself your "after midnight girl". I have now officially lost that title and am happy.

I made it to Banff yesterday with four minutes to spare, although I had to speed to get there on time. Lucky for me the police weren't out. I have to run up again tomorrow.

Once again, I am sorry to hear about your friend's passing. It only goes to show you, life can be all too short and better not to save the good times for the hereafter and learn to make the most of this world by living each day as if it were your last. Maybe that is why I tend to burn the candle at both ends.

I remember when I was younger, thinking I may not make it to thirty. I always worked and played hard. It is only 7:00 o'clock and I have put on my second pot of coffee for today. Not much appears to have changed. I cleaned out all my work files on the home computer and made a list of "to dos" for clients.

My mother is still very depressed. I went to check on them last night and she is really not doing well. She is in a great deal of pain in spite of the heavy duty painkillers her doctor has prescribed. I washed some of her clothes and she was crying the whole time. Hopefully she will snap out of this depression soon. Unfortunately, my father has to take the brunt of it.

This whole week I have been thinking again about how lucky I am with everything in life and how blessed I am. Last night I told

Joanna, this year, was the beginning of the happiest times in my life. I am now at an age where the children are almost grown and gone and where I can begin to focus more on myself. At least I can exist on my own again, which is a huge step for me. I am finally at an age, where I have garnered some wisdom and a great deal of piece of mind with who and what I am.

Unlike when I turned thirty, with all the pressures and urges of bearing children and all the inner turmoil that comes with that. Then in my forties, all I could think about was trying to be the best mother and wife I could be, the ultimate domestic. Those were very busy years for me, especially with over that period running the furniture store and later the Bed and Breakfast.

Now I have a wonderful circle of friends I can call my own. I can dance until dawn with them and then go to work. They think I should take up belly dancing and not salsa. My relationship with Joanna has turned out to be wonderfully fulfilling. The real estate is something I truly enjoy and will be financially rewarding as well and will hopefully allow me to do anything else I want to do.

Now you have come into my life and have made it much more special, by making me feel brand new. That was the only part that seemed to be missing, although I didn't realize it at the time. I have lost all this weight and can finally feel good about my body again and you have shown me that I am still able to function sexually. You have shown me that I can actually still enjoy it as ever before.

I think I understand now; I never wanted to live without it as I enjoy it far too much. My girlfriend from Toronto told me earlier this year that I was a very sensual person and I didn't really understand what she meant as I wasn't having any sex at the time. I guess all she meant was the aura of a person and what they exude. Come to think of it though, she should know as she and I did a little experiment quite a number of years ago, while I was still single. I hope you are not shocked by me telling you this, as I assume you have lived long enough to have seen a great deal, or so your stories tell me.

Julianna asked me last year if I ever had a sexual relationship with a woman before and naturally I had to be honest and told her of this brief encounter. It was only curiosity on her part and I told her that this was quite natural for most women and she should not be ashamed of these thoughts. I found it amazing she would feel comfortable enough with me to ask the question. I know it certainly isn't a question I could have asked my mother.

Isn't life interesting! You don't need to wonder where my theory on maximum exposure comes from. If we could all stop for a moment and not be so afraid of our own emotions, actions and thoughts, provided they are good, we could learn better how to live without regret. We also need to learn how to share these thoughts and accept others' thoughts with respect and tolerance. Does this make any sense to you? Besides, what is that saying, about the person to "cast the first stone"?

Now I have to get to work, but let me tell you it was difficult driving home yesterday after seeing you in Calgary and not being able to really touch you. I assume tonight is also out of the question as I know you have to set up and tear down your gear again and it will be too late for us. C'est la vie! Tomorrow is another day. I will keep my mind busy today with thoughts of you and it will be fun.

Love
Irene

P.S. I didn't mean for you to lose the "later". I liked it, as it is so much a part of you. It only took me awhile to figure out what "later" means for you as in "later" today, "later" this week or "later" this year?

Part Six
The Christmas Blues

Chapter 24

Sent: December 8, 2006 9:34 A.M.
Subject: Is anyone out there?

Good morning!

I half expected you to call last night, but no doubt Jane was keeping you guys entertained as usual. She really needs to get a life instead of showing up at all your gigs, just to hang around Chuck, Greg, you and other women's men.

I managed to sleep until 6:00 A.M. and I feel a great deal better than yesterday. In the afternoon, I had one of those power naps that everyone keeps talking about. I have to stop getting up at 5:00 A.M. By noon, I'm exhausted, especially after I have been digging into my head so early in the morning. This definitely cannot be healthy.

Great news today- I am now three pounds closer to my goal. My workouts at the gym are getting better each time. I am now up to sixty pound weights, with double the amount of time on each machine. Soon all those pounds gained during menopause will be shed! I think I will try to lose an additional five over what I first thought and that will bring me closer to my weight before children. It is so exciting; this morning I tried on one of my favourite blouses that hasn't fit since 2000 and it fits again! The only problem is, it is out of style and I no longer like it as much. I dropped it at the thrift shop, but at least it fit.

Speaking of fasting....are you still planning on spending the nights over the weekend or will you go home, with Jordon back from Montreal? I am not sure what you told Jordon and Allison about me, but I assume Allison must be wondering about where you have been the last eight weekends in a row. The reason I am asking is because you seem to be making an effort NOT to involve me in your personal life in Calgary, other than the coffee on Wednesday, which I did enjoy. No wonder I called Allison, Alicia. I have never met her and I have always been better with numbers than names..... remember Larry? My meeting your two children in Calgary is totally your choice though.

Anyway, I am on floor duty right now and I need to get back to it. I would have written from home, but the internet was down. I hope you give me reason to say thank God, it's Friday or Saturday or Thursday, for that matter. Remember Lily and Peter are coming for dinner tonight and they will probably still be there when you are finished playing.

Hope to see you later....
Irene

The simple fact that I had not yet met his children was unsettling for me. I found it very strange and it left me to wonder "why". I was accepting a behaviour I did not find normal and I was leaving myself open to a great deal of pain, if the reason turned out to be he was married. Joanna and I discussed this many times and I refused to believe someone could do that at our age. In her twenties, she had had her own experiences with a married man and they are always destructive. By this time, I believe all of my friends thought that I had fallen in love with a married man and the look on their faces was one of pity. Once I acknowledged this as a possibility, was when the bleeding began.

Sent: December 8, 2006 1:36 P.M.
Subject: Out here

Hi there,

Someone is out here of course. I suppose Jane must have been really excited last night in Banff, since we weren't there at all. I told you last weekend we were not going to Buffalo's this week because they had a private party there and we had a function in Calgary to do. We don't do Banff again until next week.

I am not in DMF tonight either. Greg and I have to play at a function in Calgary, at the Palliser so we really had to pass on DMF and hire Chuck as a guest vocalist and get him out of the fame zone of the Bow Valley and into urban performance reality.

I'm actually slowly adjusting to the fact my musical existence with its twists and turns now has a love life to adjust to, as far as scheduling is concerned. I will adjust and do I feel famine?

Will call later.......the famous......later

Luv
Cephus

Chapter 25

Sent: December 10, 2006 11:57 A.M.
Subject: Torture!

It is now 7:00 A.M. on Sunday and I am still alive! The past two days have been absolute torture! There can't be anything worse than expecting someone and then they don't show up. I actually had to cry last night, just to get rid of some of the negative energy and then I could finally fall asleep.

Please, do me a favour and the next time you tell me something, make sure I hear it. Maybe what you don't realize is that besides needing reading glasses, I am also getting hard of hearing. Just look me in the eyes and make absolutely certain I understand and hear.

We have gotten into a regular routine of at least Friday and Saturday nights and when you didn't call or show up on Friday night, I was lost, because I hadn't heard you tell me you weren't going to be out here. In fact, I was thinking you told me the opposite and we were going to have two weekends of feasting.

All day yesterday, I found I could barely function, thinking of you. Maybe it was the four hours of sleep. What I do know is by the end of last night, someone could have taken needles and stuck them under my fingernails and that would have been less painful.

There is a big difference between feast, famine and that word I don't like…… "Whoa"! I know I can live without having sex for a very long time and not think anything of it. Then when I am involved sexually with someone, I need it quite regularly and definitely more than just once a week or I begin to think I will go insane without it. It is like waving candy in front of a child and then you don't give it to them. How cruel is that? It is like I always said, "It's either all or nothing, not 'whoa' and just now and again". I can't deal with rationing, when it comes to sex. It's not healthy for my body or my mind.

A number of times over the last forty-eight hours, I truly thought you were just playing games with me and were carrying the anticipation thing to the max. It reminded me of the same game the Swiss guy used to play. The only problem is this is how I wound up dating first two and then three men at the same time. This is not somewhere I want to go at this stage in my life.

The last two days almost pushed me over the edge as I found myself thinking about emailing the Austrian doctor who's been waiting for something to happen to John, for six years now. He has been phoning and emailing and he now knows that John is gone. I have been worried he will show up at my door, uninvited.

Last night my mother again told me that this man I know in Banff still keeps asking about me and yesterday he told her that he hoped she would win on the VLTS, enough to pay for our wedding. I wonder, what in God's name is in his head, as we only had one date in high school.

I will not have a problem saving my energy for you as long as you don't put me on rations and make me go for days on end without seeing you, touching you, talking to you and, of course, having you inside of me.

When you see me tonight, you will notice I am now withering away and I have lost even more weight and my doctor and parents have told me to stop.

Sooner...rather than...later!
Irene

Cephus's theory on anticipation entailed how love and life should be taken slowly and savoured. To a certain extent, I did agree, but certainly not when it came to the frequency of loving another and being together. I certainly felt loved by him when we were together; however, when too many days elapsed without hearing or seeing him, I would question his love. The doubt in my mind about his current marital status began to plague me even more, but I couldn't bare the thought of not seeing him again. I started to count down the days when I would see him next.

Chapter 26

Sent: December 12, 2006 7:03 A.M.
Subject: A Big Thank You, From Your Girl in Canmore

What a wonderfully relaxing day, yesterday! Thank you so very much. You see how simple life really is. All the turmoil of Friday and Saturday vanished and all it took was one night with you. Never underestimate the power of sexual gratification.

I got used to being sexually satisfied two days a week and when it didn't happen, my mind and body revolted. There were no emotions of jealousy, anger, fear or any of those others, only pure sexual frustration.

Yesterday I enjoyed a tranquil mind and body all day. In fact, that one night with you should last me until Friday now. The only thing I have to be careful of all week is that I can't think of what you said to me while you were lying on me (the one occasion) or I will get all worked up again. Your words popped into my head a couple of times yesterday and I started to get all excited again. I quickly banished the thought so as not to disturb the peacefulness of the day.

Did Jordon arrive safe and sound yesterday? You will have a wonderful few weeks with him home again. I can understand you wouldn't want to go anywhere with me while he is with you. So don't be afraid to tell me you don't want to go anywhere on the 26th. We can go somewhere after he returns to Montreal. You still haven't told me what your schedule is like that week and I would like to know, as I will be alone. If possible, I would like to spend more time with you. Please let me know what your plans are.

When I arrived at work yesterday, I found Beth in the back office crying. She is pregnant and will not tell her family and friends until after the first trimester is over. She is worried it would upset them, if something happens. You see how people are afraid of opening up. Why would she want to suffer through this on her own, should something really happen? She is so emotionally worked up and desperately needs to share this with her family and friends. If something goes wrong, at least she will have this big circle of loved ones to support her. I think it is never wrong to share one's true feelings, as it more often than not, brings us closer together as people.

After hugs, I told her to go home and get some rest and I finished her shift. She left, not quite happy, but more at peace with herself because she had shared her secret with me.

Good thing we made love about four times yesterday as I should get four days of productive work out of it and will be all right until Friday. What I wanted to ask you yesterday and didn't get out was I wanted to know what your plans were for Christmas day. Are both Jordon and Allison with you that day? Would the three of you, like to join the three of us for dinner? Of course, I would need to invite Franky and his father as I always manage to find a few strays at Christmas. I don't need to make a turkey as Julianna and Danny are not that fond of turkey either. You still haven't told me if you have kept me a secret from your children. Maybe you operate under the same theory as Beth for fear of something going wrong. Fear not!

Now Cephus, you will notice that in this email there are a number of question marks as there were in so many other emails I have sent. It would be nice if, once in awhile, I would get an answer to some of these questions, unless the questions are too difficult to answer.

Another time, I will gather up all the unanswered ones and put them all in one email. That could be a difficult day for you as there will be far too many at once for you to respond to. Maybe you should quit procrastinating and start on some of them now. Remember, regardless of what the answers are, the choices you make are yours and ours to live with.

Love you!
Irene

P.S. Maybe I will try putting the "I" in front of the "Love" again and see what happens. Yes, I got up again this morning just after 5.

Maybe I just like birds.

Chapter 27

The big question of whether or not Cephus was married now became an open and major topic of discussion between my family and friends. They saw the angst it created in me. Was this the real reason for never inviting me to his home and meeting his children? Cephus could not see the importance or relevance of the question because, in his mind, he had already answered it in the beginning of the relationship. What he failed to understand was the simple fact that, in anyone's opinion and most importantly in my mind, his secrecy and actions did not match his words.. His words did not remove the doubt and suspicion and, to the contrary, it was left to burn and fester in my heart.

The last email from Cephus was written on the 5th and his emails became fewer and further between, similar to his phone calls. Christmas was fast approaching and the prospects of spending it alone began to wear me down and it threw me into quite an emotional state. The less I heard from him, the more anxiety it produced. I would go from a total calm and inner peace, when I was with him, to an anxious state when he wasn't with me and I didn't hear from him. I knew I had the power to change this and I questioned why I was giving it to him when I knew better. His reasoning was I was only looking for a replacement for John, which I couldn't see.

December was always his busiest time of year. I knew he could have as many as three gigs in a day, leading up to Christmas, with all the company parties, private functions as well as his regular gigs. This was not even taking into consideration all the extra travel time involved to get from one place to another and to set up and dismantle his equipment. I understood this, but I wanted him to make time for me, if I was important to him.

It is difficult to fight the fear of being unwanted or unloved and that is exactly what was happening. I had just experienced all these similar emotions with John's leaving and now here I was dealing with them all over again. I knew the children and I were much better off not having to put up with the emotional highs and lows with John, but as happy as I was after the separation, my feelings of being loved and left still needed to be dealt with.

I wrote two more emails that day in hopes of driving him out of my system and regaining control of my emotions.

Sent: December 13, 2006 7:05 A.M.
Subject: Yours

When are you thinking of retiring? I know you have told me many times unlike others, what you do is "play" and not "work". I guess the answer to that question would be, never. The only problem with your playing is you have so little time for anything else. I'll be thinking of you and your hectic day tomorrow.

Whatever happened to that laid back, slow moving Caribbean attitude I know? That is one of the things I really liked about the cultures of the Caribbean and the South Pacific. I always thought that the Western world could learn a great deal from this and could slow down. Sometimes we should stop and ask ourselves what it is we are chasing. What is it we think we want and need in life in order to be happy?

The one thing I have thought and said many times in the past is there is such a big difference between what a person actually needs in life versus what a person merely wants. If we could only learn to separate and distinguish between the two, we would be much better off. There is far too much confusion going on, with respects to what we perceive as being the necessities of life. In fact, if we could understand this better, then maybe more women would stay home to raise and nurture their children, our only hope for the future.

In my mind, it would not reverse the liberation of women as we do have a choice on whether or not to bear children or establish a career in the first place. Once we have made the decision to have children, then I think it is in society's best interests that someone be home to teach, feed and love them. Or do we just leave it to strangers, nurseries and teachers? How can we possibly expect these people to nurture our children as well as we can? Who is really missing out here and what exactly is more important in life, our children or the sailboat in the drive we cannot afford?

One only has to look at the obesity that now exists in North America and wonder why. Women have thrown themselves into the work force thinking the extra income is actually needed, when, in fact, it isn't. Now they find themselves in a situation, where they have no time to prepare nutritional meals and the age of fast food takes hold. Making things from scratch is much healthier, rewarding and fun and, in the end, saves a great deal of money. Ultimately, it becomes apparent that a family can live quite nicely on one income. I am almost certain this house was always full of adults and children passing through because of the abundant and seemingly endless supply of homemade food and at so little cost, except my labour and we don't want to add that up.

I have to run now, but at least you know I have started my day, with you in my thoughts.

Yours truly....sincerely yours......or just plain YOURS!

Irene

Sent: December 13, 2006 9:46 A.M.
Subject: Full or Running on Empty

On the way into Banff this morning it finally dawned on me why God meant for us to connect. You are supposed to show me the way back to a place in time, before wife and motherhood. I remember your words, about how you didn't want the wife or mother part of me and all you wanted was the woman. I was confused at the time as I know you never had the mother in bed. As for the wife, the "woman" under you is not the wife of the last eighteen years. Really, what you are getting is the person I almost forgot and didn't think existed anymore. I understand better now, what you were talking about, but I do still need more time in order to perfect this new me. You can let me know when I have arrived.

Now for what I think God intended for me to give to you. As soon as the words "slow moving Caribbean attitude" hit the paper, a light went on. I think you have definitely become Canadianized and have possibly forgotten your roots! You have totally forgotten how to have fun or do something for yourself, other than your music. You are always too busy running here and there playing, trying to bring enjoyment into other peoples' lives and never thinking about your own and those who love you.

Maybe it is because you have become too cynical over the years with all those relationships that had gone wrong. You told me this once in the beginning so it is not something I have made up. On the other hand, I am not cynical! I don't care how many relationships I have in my life or what becomes of them. I will always be happy in the end and with the people around me at that time.

In the beginning of our relationship, my parents were concerned I may get hurt and they told me to be careful. My answer to them was that I wasn't going to stop living nor change the way I lived my life for fear of getting hurt. I never did in the past and why, at my age now, would I want to start? My theory is caution belongs in the wind. All I had to tell them was, if the last eighteen years didn't get me depressed or cynical, nothing in life ever would. They agreed.

Now, back to you and the day you have planned for yourself tomorrow. I know the perfect tune and the words could have been written for you. The song, of course, is by the Eagles, "Running on Empty. Does this strike a chord with you?

You tell me you don't take vacations or time off and I am wondering when and if you will run out of gas and especially at your age. This is not what I would consider the standard personality trait of someone from the Caribbean. Nor is this the personality trait I admired throughout my travels in my younger years. Whatever happened to variety being the spice of life? I thought you were from the land of spice.

You will have to start taking more time off, if these emails start getting shorter rather than longer. The problem I have in making them shorter is that we are trying to have a relationship based on seeing each other twice a week between midnight and morning and what generally occurs between those hours.

The whole purpose of being able to spend some time together, during the course of a day or on a DATE, is to talk about things in life. I wonder if anything has changed for me from all those years of talking to the stove, sink or washer. Oh yes, I am not talking to myself and you are reading these emails.

I don't want a relationship with you based solely on sex, although it is ABSOLUTELY WONDERFUL! I promised you before you were not going to be my "toy boy" and I don't want to just be your, "after midnight girl".

What would you like for Christmas? I do want to get you something, but I am stuck. All I want for Christmas is you! Isn't that a tune? Actually, I thought of a great idea last night. Why don't we just exchange dates? You take me out somewhere doing something and then another day I will take you out somewhere, doing something and no sex until you're favourite, later, and nice and slow. Doesn't that sound like a good idea?

Now you can see all the questions in this one, but just answer the last one and I will be happy. Now I am not going to send you another thing until next week. I promise!

The long winded me.

Irene

P.S. Everyone at work is wondering why there has been a smile on my face all week. Little do they know I am keeping myself entertained again with those four little words you left me with on Monday morning and at least you know it doesn't take much to please me.

Sent: December 13, 2006 3:08 P.M.
Subject: On Geniuses of any description

You remind me so much of one of my cousins. He is the mathematical genius of the family. I remember him telling me years ago about how absolutely everything in life revolved around or was related to a mathematical equation. The only problem with his theory was regardless of his genius, he always seemed to have difficulty relating to people and in particular with his relationships. I am certain he could not fathom a life without the equation and no one expects this of him. He dated a girlfriend of mine from Trinidad for quite awhile and she ultimately left him because he did not know how to really enjoy life. He could not take his head out of the equation long enough.

A friend of John's from New York had a similar philosophy in life and never took time off his medical career to enjoy time with his wife. Early in our marriage, they had spent some time with us and I listened to her story on being married to a genius. He also never figured it out until long after she left. Who knows, he may still not quite grasp it. The last thing I heard was that at age fifty-four he was still seeking a wife and children.

I won't get into another cousin of mine who is a neurologist and onto, I think, the third wife. None of these three geniuses knew how to take time away from their careers to actually enjoy other aspects of life. Do you see any similarity between these people and you? You are the musical genius who also appears to be single- minded when it comes to enjoyment of life.

Compare it to having sex missionary style for your entire life and never experiencing the thrill of all those other positions. How boring would that be? I shouldn't end this with thinking of all those positions. Talk about single- mindedness and I have been doing so well this week.

Thank you again for phoning just now. It was nice to hear your voice too. The call I missed was from a private number and they didn't leave a message. I hope I haven't lost a sale. C'est la vie. There's more to life than just selling houses.

Can we do that chair thing again on the weekend?

Love
Irene

Sent: December 13, 2006 4:01 P.M.
Subject: Are you still there?

Okay, maybe all you need in your life is your piano. Somehow I get a different impression. When we are in bed together, it seems you have other needs as well. The last thing that I would expect is for you to retire! That would be a real shame. All I have said is I would like for you to slow down and take more time to look after some of your other needs as well as the needs of your loved ones and to be able to enjoy other aspects of human existence.

Irene

Chapter 28

Sent: December 13, 2006 10:54 P.M.
Subject: ???????????

Hi there Irene,

I read your emails today over and over a few times and I struggled for awhile to contain my irritation at the tone of the communiqués....

What happened to the guy you met? What's wrong with him? So you think you can get into his head and change who he is with negativity?

This was previously going to be a long tirade about that but I decided not to send it because it sounded angry and I really am not but suffice it to say that I am comfortable in my own skin and I have a lot of interests outside of music and I'm not bitter or screwed up as you seem to be implying and you are not going to change me. All it would do is ruin, what we are building. It will take another sixty-three years for that to happen.

Luv
Cephus

Sent: December 14, 2006 8:52 A.M.
Subject: Re: ????????

Irritation was the last thing I expected! If it was all hogwash, all you had to do is say "Bull"?! And correct me. I am certainly not trying to change you and bitter and screwed up is NOT the way I perceive you. It was more a hypothetical question. I am not involved with your life in the city. Does he or does he not do other things in life besides play the piano? How, in God's name, would I know the

life besides play the piano? How, in God's name, would I know the answer to that? All I know is it certainly hasn't been with me.

The whole thing has only to do with the fact that after two months of us seeing each other; my world and the people in it think this relationship is just another one of my good stories and a figment of my imagination. The mystery man still remains just that, a mystery to everyone, including me.

You have this whole other life out there, which I know nothing about and, apparently, you are happy with me not knowing because I have never heard of two people seeing each other for over two months and they have only shared one cup of coffee together in the daylight.

I have no idea what your favourite color is or what your favourite food is, much less what, if anything, you do when you are not playing your piano. I fail to see, how my asking you these questions, could be perceived as negative or me trying to change you. I only want to get to know you better and I am having a difficult time doing that, when there is so little time together.

You have gotten into my head because I willingly let you in and have allowed you to muck about with it and I am content with that, to a certain degree. You have told me all about your perceptions of women and how you know what they are like after a divorce and you have put me in the same boat with the rest of them. I have never been remotely upset by your analogies and, on the contrary, I have found your stories amusing; whether they fit me or not is irrelevant. I love listening to you talk! I could have just as easily taken your stories of how women are, including me, after their husbands have left them and turned it into something negative, but I chose not to.

So are you so upset now, you will cancel on me Friday night or can we discuss this further in person, tomorrow? By the way, the tone in which I wrote everything, was a happy one. I was in an extremely good mood yesterday.

I really hope your busy day goes smoothly and I haven't upset you enough to screw things up between us. This is the last thing I intended to do. If either of us was looking for something different, we wouldn't be talking right now. We are too old for that.

I love you just the way you are!
Irene

Thank God my computer crashed after this email. I told the technician there was no rush to fix it and I would pick it up the following week. I no longer wanted a computer at home and I looked forward to the mental break from last week's seemingly endless discussions with myself. We do have six computers in the office and maybe that is why I stayed away from there for the next two days.

By Sunday I wound up back at work staring at a computer. Looking down at the keyboard, I decided to implement a new plan of action. I would just keep typing my thoughts without hitting send and who knew, I may decide never to send them and keep them for myself. Could this be me playing hard to get and pushing his buttons?

Chapter 29

Subject: Dreams and Things

Sunday Morning

Now it is Sunday and Chris has called me to cover floor duty for him again. On Sundays there are so few people around looking over my shoulder. This is bad news for me, but good for you?!? I just couldn't resist the temptation so here I am again, typing.

Forget all question marks from now on. I promised myself I wasn't going to ask you any more questions, at least not this year anymore. By the way, I have also decided that you don't need to answer any of the two hundred and seventeen asked so far and that you haven't replied to. Answers to those don't matter anymore. I have decided to make them irrelevant as waiting for answers is far too torturous, breaks my spirit and I don't want my spirit tampered with. Suffice it to say, I have never before invited someone to Christmas dinner and not received a "yes" or a "no". The invitation, of course, is cancelled. I am sure you will enjoy your dinner with family and/ or friends of your world, unless, of course, you have no intentions of eating anything on Christmas Day.

I need to tell you about some dreams I have been having in the past number of weeks, both at night and when I am awake. All too often, I find myself dreaming of the two of us walking somewhere, holding hands, sitting somewhere, holding hands and a quiet place with soft music playing in the background, with your arms around me and holding me tight. I have dreamt about us surrounded by warm water and the sun beating down and, of course, we are in each other's arms. All of these dreams make me feel so good inside, not only in my body, but in my mind as well. The thoughts produce such tranquility that I am always hesitant to disturb them, to get on with the day.

Please don't take this the wrong way, but without you knowing it, you have been extinguishing these dreams one by one. Like blowing candles out that are burning for you. Like most women, I need these dreams and hopes, because I just do. You know there are many differences between the male and female psyche and this is one of them. I don't think it's necessary to analyze it to death and we should be satisfied with just saying that if it makes one feel good about themselves and those around them, it can't be much of a bad thing.

Over the past few weeks, each time I have mentioned one of these dreams and suggested we do something together, you have basically told me you have been there and done that and really, why bother doing them again. I have found myself feeling foolish for even having the dreams, which is not right. You are snuffing out the flames of my love, leaving me to think that there really isn't anything left for us to do together, at least not in the daylight hours. You seem to have lost the desire to do any of these things, which you have done in the past, so many times and with so many other women. It reminds me, when we were first married and the first time I bought a mushy card for John. His initial response was his first wife used to buy cards like that and I needn't bother. Needless to say, it was the last mushy card he ever received from me and the rest of my cards were dull.

Now I find myself at the same crossroads in life. Do I stop dreaming like I did with John or do I carry on in my own little world, in spite of what you say or do not do? Do I need to change again now so soon after the last? I am reluctant as I know this one will come at a heftier price, not having fully recovered from the last. My astrological sign indicates I am the zodiac's best chameleon, but, regardless, it can at times prove extremely difficult. In the past, one of the methods I used to make the transition from one dream world with one love in my life was to take on another and another and, in this, I have found the strength to move on. I did try to tell you this before and now I find myself desperate to get out of town, which is not often a good sign for me. Will I be looking? No, but sometimes I am discovered just the same.

It is not really you who needs to change, but me. I had dinner at Joanna's last night and she had an old friend visiting. After dinner Joanna attended a Christmas function for a short while and left the two of us to watch "Holly". I kept thinking how wonderful it felt to be with friends, have dinner and then just sit and talk afterwards. The conversation was varied, interesting and without emotion, other than relaxing. The only problem is that the whole evening I couldn't help, but wonder why you and I couldn't share an evening like that together, with me in this world or with you in yours.

Today I have come to the conclusion that you must have, some-where along your way, surrounded yourself with an immense brick wall, when it comes to women. I can see it now and it is extreme-ly high and virtually impenetrable. I believe construction of this wall began shortly after your marriage failed and it has continued throughout the years with the multitude of women who have come and gone since.

You are deathly afraid of opening yourself and your world up to me. It appears you have had enough of us women. All you are pre-pared to share are stories of your past, your philosophies and your analogies of life, but you are not prepared to share the present, other than those brief moments in conversation before and after sex.

How sad to think I am only in your life to fulfill your sexual urges, as anything else would be just too complicated for you. I was so busy dreaming my dreams and living in my own world I actually didn't see it until the previous paragraph. In my own words, lay the answers to all my questions. The only problem with this realization is that there are still too many contradictions with you.

You won't allow me to really get under your skin, by keeping me at arm's length from your world and this is your choice and I can accept this. On the other hand, now and again you keep tossing me these little bones to chew on.. Your email last Thursday, for exam-ple, said something about building our relationship and, on another occasion, I recall you saying something about how tough your skin was and you don't give up easily on your women. And, oh yes, there was the email where you indicated you were having to see about fitting a love life into your busy schedule. What really confuses me is the fact you actually went through all my emails and counted the number of my questions that went unanswered. I had to ask myself: if I were only there to fulfill your sexual needs, then why would you have wasted so much time on the arithmetic? All this leaves me to think; what is it exactly we are building and what difference does it make how tough your skin is, if you are not interested in having me under it? This is not a question for you, but for me.

I suppose having to spend Friday and Saturday nights with me is one giant step for you. Believe me, when I say there are no words to describe how much I enjoy having you here on those nights, but greedy as most humans are, I find it a long week and come Sunday night, I only wish you were back again on Monday. Instead, what I have to look forward to, is usually not a word from you until Friday night again.

The dreams and thoughts of you in my head were the only things nurturing me all week in your absence. Now here I almost wrote something I never do. I almost wrote the words, "I wish and I wish you wouldn't take the dreams from me".

What a mistake that would have been as I so much dislike the use of the word and rarely do I use it. I don't usually wish for anything as I find it to be such a waste of time and energy. I either get what I need and want and if I find I can't have it, I go on to the next thing. As for you taking the dreams from me, I have them back again because I refuse to give them up at this time. So they have only been gone a few days.

I have to run now.

Love
Irene

Sunday Evening

I had to break and go to another work- related Christmas open house. I assumed it would be a small gathering, but it turned out to be about fifty people, most of whom I knew. I was not in the right frame of mind for it, but I managed just fine. There were many people I hadn't seen in a long time so that was nice. The food was not very good, but the conversation was enjoyable, as usual. I avoided spending too much time with the guys and wound up focusing on other women and they were happy to unload. I listened to their mostly sad tales and too many were curious to know about who was occupying my time lately.

Naturally I told them a "bit" about you as that is all I know so far. I have a feeling they know how open I am to life and they are suspicious when I don't say very much. I usually prefer to remain obscure at these functions, but I think there has been too drastic a change in my outer appearance this past year and I felt like all eyes were upon me. I did not feel comfortable and I left early. I am sure this is another change I will get used to, the leaving early part.

Now, I would like to continue with my ever hopeful, demolition of the wall I think surrounds you. Consider once, how long it's taken you to pile on the bricks and mortar and to make absolutely certain no one can break through and how this could prove to be a daunting task, with a likelihood of failure on my part. I feel that it is absolutely necessary, however, to make the attempt.

One of the major differences between us is that, regardless of the baggage and the past demands that I may have to battle through with this divorce, I do have the ability to drop one thing and go onto the next. Rather than deal with the villain, I can choose to ignore him and get on with my chameleon life. I can "work a room" and pick someone else to listen to and be thankful for the distraction. I need only to become them and get out of my own skin for awhile.

When I am listening to someone tell me a story of his/her life, I feel like this individual is giving me a piece of his/her soul and I am allowed to feel like I am a part of this person. I begin to feel so connected to this person; if I am cut off from the story, I feel like I have just lost a finger. Maybe this is the reason why I can listen so well to people of all ages. It allows me to be all ages, at all times before actually being there or being there again, after already having been there. Possibly, is this the discovery of eternal youth or eternal agedness?

Talk to you later. Love you!

I felt it necessary to add this part about listening. Cephus told me on a number of occasions that I wasn't listening and I could not understand why. The one thing I loved to do was to listen to him and he was accusing me of not loving to listen to him, which hurt. I knew all his stories by heart; and how could I possibly do this if I wasn't paying attention? Besides, in my mind, I often found it difficult to get a word in. I would open my mouth to respond to something and this is when he would tell me I wasn't listening. Soon, it became a habit for me to bite my tongue and save everything for my emails. On those occasions when I couldn't keep quiet, was generally the time when we fought.

Chapter 30

Monday Morning

I had to stop writing and run over to Joanna's again. She called and needed to talk about Gareth. He had spent the last fourteen hours in his room and wouldn't come out. I asked her again why his suitcase wasn't at the door and she still couldn't bring herself to end it; but then who are we to judge? I told her that for Christmas I was planning to give her one of my infamous letters, all about her and, unlike with Gareth, everything written in it would be about all the wonderful things I could think to say about her and there would be many. She put on one of her big smiles. I know my gift will make her happy this Christmas. That would be a better gift, coming straight from the heart, than say, a candle or bath soaps.

The children got home from Calgary about 10:00 o'clock last night and John had cancelled the trip to Vancouver for them. I have to phone Joanna this morning and let her know I can't leave the country now. I will have to go to plan "B" and whatever that means. Maybe I will start tearing the house apart and get it ready to sell.

Everyone in the house slept in this morning, including me. I didn't wake up until 8:00 o'clock, which was such a treat for me. You see how relaxed I have become without the computer in the house. I was going to pick it up today, but I should leave it a "bit" longer. The only problem is Danny and Julianna need it for their school work. I really should quit procrastinating and pick it up today. This morning I need to finish my Christmas mail to clients so I need to go.

I will continue later.

Monday Afternoon

I am tired of doing Christmas mail. Now I have completed forty-three and I am not even close to being finished. I wish I could have been happy with a generic greeting, instead of having to personalize all of them. Leave it to me to choose the path of most resistance.

I forgot to tell you this morning I woke up at 8:00 o'clock and really didn't want to get out of bed. All I could smell was your cologne. I used your pillow, instead of mine, for a change. Please don't change this on my account, the cologne, that is. It could confuse me into thinking someone else had been in my bed and I quite like it anyway.

I asked Joanna last night what she thought I should get you for Christmas. I am so stumped. You don't want me to get behind this brick wall of yours or truly under your skin. I told Joanna I should get you something totally impersonal, like a pair of socks or a tie. She asked me if you wear ties and I said, "Of course not". Anything, mushy or personal and I have a feeling you will bring out the mortar again. Once again you seem to be making my life difficult.

A bit later.

Monday Night

Getting back to my discussion with you yesterday about this wall you want no one to penetrate……mmmmm, now that is an interesting word and definitely one of my favourites. There are many problems with not allowing people to penetrate or to get under the skin. So much of life has a tendency of being too superficial, if we don't allow anyone in. It could be you are trying, but you don't really know how or you are just too busy fighting with yourself about the when and how much of a relationship you can handle at this time. You must have noticed by now that I also have a stubborn streak and how, like you, I am not easily throwing in the towel and giving up on this relationship. That is why I will keep my dreams, regardless of what you say and do.

Just think of all the money I have saved myself in psychiatric fees over the years, by being so open with people. Did you know that the more you keep things bottled up inside, the higher the risk of mental illness? Maybe this is why I don't really think I have a whole lot of baggage from the marriage, in spite of what you may think. I think the world would be a far better place, if we would allow ourselves to open up and be less guarded about our lives and our feelings. We should learn to let go of the fear of the discovery of some personal secret. If we do this, we may find that, in most cases, the listener has already been there or experienced something similar or knows someone who has. Here we may find the thread that allows people to actually connect and have a better understanding of one another and, in turn, more tolerance.

I have another theory on why you have been secretive about your world and not wanting me to see any of it. It could be you are not sure of what I would think if I found out you watched only sports, CNN or too many cartoons on television. The reason I mention cartoons is from what I have noticed; it takes you too many seconds to switch from the cartoon to the sport. This makes me think that if I wasn't in the room, you would leave it on that station for awhile longer than what you would want others to notice.

What would I think if I accidently found out that this brilliant musician was actually just a regular guy who left the toilet seat up all the time? What if he lives in "la-la-land" and is the type to fart on your leg after sex and then fall asleep? I have caught more than a glimpse of these "flaws" of human nature and I haven't batted an eye.

I need to wrap this up and go home. It's 9:30 P.M. and it's been a busy evening. My ninety-two year old client returned from Arizona yesterday and invited me to tea for 3:30 this afternoon. I didn't get there until after 4:00 and first I drove to pick up a parcel of hers. When we got back to her place, she asked if I wanted the usual tea or would I like a different drink for a change. I asked her what she had in mind besides tea, she replied, "How's a Vodka"? She seemed to be happy when I agreed to join her.

This did confirm my earlier suspicions about her. I helped her unpack all her worldly possessions some months ago, when she first arrived in Canmore. I had no idea where or what happened to all her children, grandchildren and great-grandchildren. All I knew was that from her arrival day in Canmore until weeks later, not a soul was in sight to help her get unpacked and get organized, other than me. When I hung up her sexy dresses from years ago, that was my first clue. It was easy for me to imagine her in her younger years and going out with the girls; and this would explain the glint in her eyes. I thought the glint had less to do with the fact she is legally blind and more to do with her strong spirit. She was disappointed I couldn't stay for a second drink, but I would almost bet this didn't stop her.

From there, I went over to feed the children and then on to my parents. My father called during dinner, wondering why they hadn't seen me since Saturday. Joanna joined us there for awhile and then it was off to the gym for me. Now I am finally going home to bed and will most likely be using your pillow again.

The good news is that I did pick up my computer today. I get to finally decide what to do with all this that I have written. The best thing is that I don't need to run to work every time something jumps into my head. Now I can actually go down to the computer and type it when I have my pyjamas on.

Much later.

Monday Night (Cont. at home)

It appears there is still a problem with this computer. No naked women have jumped up on the screen, but Norton is telling me there is still some kind of problem. I will try to fix this myself tomorrow. Though, the unfortunate thing is that your last email from the 8th was there for me to read once more, when I opened Outlook. That was the week of such disappointments. First, you wind up not playing Buffalo's and then you wind up not playing Benny's, both Friday and Saturday nights. You say you told me, but I certainly didn't catch it.

When I got home tonight, I made everyone a huge bowl of fruit and then finished making the Kampuchea. Everyone appears to be content for the time being. I can't imagine how people can enter into any type of a relationship without expecting some sort of change. This is coming from the making of Kampuchea all these years, which is so reliant on chemical changes that occur in its life. With the making of Kampuchea, some form of natural change must take place and the drink gains effervescence and if it doesn't, then you wind up with something you may as well toss. I liken the drink to love and life.

I need to go to bed now as I have to pick up Janis, the ninety-two year old, and take her to the bus at 8:40 A.M. and then on to my staff meeting. Lily and Peter are taking me to lunch tomorrow and will try to convince me to go to Mexico or elsewhere over the holidays. I'll listen to what they have to say.

Done, good night.

Tuesday Evening

I am in the office again this afternoon and I met a nice couple from Toronto. They have been watching our market for two years now and they look like they could be good prospects. Wish me luck. Oh, I forgot, I'm not giving you this until next week.

I always believed women deserved equal treatment to men and I was happy we finally got the vote. It really isn't nice waiting for things like phone calls, emails, or dates and sex. Now that was nasty. Please get over it.

I didn't get to bed until 2:00 o'clock this morning and, needless to say, I was not up at my usual 5:00 A.M., but I slept until 7:50. Panic... because I had to drive the kids to school, pick up Janis and drop her at the bus and attend the staff meeting by 9:00. I was thirty seconds late. The new owner was at the meeting this morning and now he probably thinks that I'm a bumble brain. I am not worried as he will soon find out I am not.

I had a great lunch with Lily and Peter in Banff today and they still did not convince me to leave the kids home alone and go off somewhere over Christmas. It is unfortunate if I don't, as it has been over twenty years since I've been anywhere without husband or children. I think I will be far too busy next week to leave anyway. Joanna is really disappointed and she keeps phoning me every day, to see if I will change my mind. Well, I still have a couple of days for things to possibly change.

You see, change can be a good and anticipated thing in life. It does not always have a bad connotation.

That's it for today.

Chapter 31

Sent: December 21, 2006 8:30 A.M.
Subject: I MISS YOU

I MISS YOU!

Love
Irene

Sent: December 21, 2006 1:34 P.M.
Subject: Died?

Have you died and gone to heaven????????????? Now this is a question?

I couldn't stand it anymore and I sent these two brief messages with the last going unsigned. By this time, I had gone a whole week and was suffering from serious withdrawal from the send button.

He called to ask why I stopped writing and if I was trying to push his buttons. All I could think of was the stupid send button and how I HADN'T pushed it all week. He asked if I was trying to torture him and if so, it wasn't going to work. After this call, I had to write again. I didn't want to be painted with the same brush as the rest of his women.

Sent: December 21, 2006 11:20 P.M.
Subject: No Torture from this end

I am sorry if my not writing has caused you any grief this week. I hope it is not why you caught a bug and are sick. I am not into torture! I have been extremely busy like you and I assure you it was..... intentional. You told me last weekend you printed all my emails that I have written so far. That really threw me off, as I have bound the whole package in a nice musical note ribbon and this was to be your Christmas gift. Now I am trying to figure something else out, at the last minute, besides trying to accumulate more emails that you haven't received and printed.

When you told me you added up all the questions in those emails, you spoiled my Christmas surprise. I have actually not stopped writing since last week. I just haven't sent them to you. I should have about twelve pages together by the time I am finished. If I wind up going away for Christmas, at least you will have something new to read while I am away. Either way, the emails belong to you and I am only withholding these for awhile. I will give them to you with your other Christmas gift. With the help of others, I did finally figure out what to get for you.

Somewhere along the way in this relationship I did get the impression you enjoyed my emails and, what a mistake, as I really know how to dish them out. I just don't know how to do things halfway and it appears it has to be "all or nothing" again. What a philosophy and a way to live!

I have missed you terribly this week, with me not being able to hit send and you never call until the last minute and you are due to come out. I think the torture has really been mine, in avoiding the "send" button. I need to go to bed now as I have to be at my mother's by 7:00 A.M. to wash and do her hair. I have to pick up clients at 8:40 A.M. for showings. They will write an offer within the next two days so it should be worth it, but still a long weekend before I am finished.

Please don't tell me you will be too sick to stop by tomorrow night, as it would totally break my heart. The funny thing is that twice yesterday they played on the car radio that Joplin song, "Take another little piece of my heart". That was twice on one trip to Banff, which I found strange as it was on the same station. It certainly wasn't a good omen for me. If you really need another little piece of my heart, help yourself as there is plenty to go around.

I miss you really badly tonight! Thank God it is Tuesday.

Miss you

Love
Irene

Chapter 32

Now it is Wednesday morning and I AM running on empty. I can't imagine how I will get everything done this week. I was in the office all day yesterday until just after 6:00 and still didn't get everything done. I have a ton of stuff I need to do today and I am getting a late start.

Actually I slept at Joanna's last night. I was not happy with Julianna and Danny so I got my PJs and told them I was running away from home. I can't get Julianna to the gym, even though I have changed her schedule twice now to suit her and she still isn't going. What a waste of money. I still haven't figured out how to get either one of them to do anything around the house. This, of course, is my entire fault as I have never asked them to do anything in the past. It is a little late to start now.

The two of them ignore things, like overflowing garbage and all that wonderful domestic stuff. All those years they were growing up, they never slept in an unmade bed and there was never a sock on their bedroom floor. I can't look at their rooms now anymore, much less walk in there. I am a neat freak and do not function well in a mess.

On Monday I forgot to tell you when I was talking about Bowness that that is where my girlfriend from Trinidad lived when they were still in Calgary. Wouldn't it be funny if her daughter, Ayoka, and Allison played ringette together?

I will have to get the kids to put up our tree tonight because I will be working until at least 9:00 and tomorrow night I doubt I will finish before 10:00 P.M. I was supposed to go to Banff tonight and tomorrow night. Lily found out that there are five plane loads of Brits who just arrived for a week of skiing. They are one of our primary markets for real estate in Canmore. The three of us were supposed to do Running Bull's these two nights for a couple of hours so I could do some networking. I am certain I would not have come up empty. Instead, I am showing property to the Toronto couple which is just as good. Maybe I can squeeze in some time on Friday night before you arrive.

Getting back to the equality of the sexes; I think this is why most women like Tina Turner and most men don't. The thought is lost because I had to go and then, accidentally started a new email. So this appears to be done.

Love and Miss You

Wednesday Evening

I have about six minutes before I meet these clients. I just got back from the gym and a very brief visit with my parents. They are quite upset that I haven't had much time for them this past week. Hopefully, I will be caught up by Friday and then I can relax a bit, but that is my mother's bingo night so they won't even be home. Though she will be happy if I at least do her hair before the bingo.

I better not waste these minutes on bingo. The reason I found myself in front of this stupid computer again is because on the way back from dropping Julianna at the gym (Yah!), all I could think about, was today is the middle of the week and I still haven't heard from you. It is easy to see who is missing whom. I suppose, for you, withdrawal symptoms from these emails is not so bad after all. I anticipated they would be, but then I am not always right.

Anyway, I miss you a great deal and in spite of how busy I am, I too often find myself thinking of you. I finally picked up your gift today. Yesterday, Lily and Peter helped me decide on it. Yes, I changed my mind.

Joanna is still searching for accommodations in Mexico and I still haven't said for certain I would not go. Julianna and Danny were much better today, since I have moved back in. They actually are making attempts at changing some of their bad habits. There is that "changing" word again. Actually my father says if we are not adaptable as people, life can be more difficult and we all know that is true.

Will be back soon

Wednesday Later

The showings went well and they will view the other five properties tomorrow. They CHANGED their schedule and want me to try and move the evening showings to the afternoon. Now I will have to CHANGE my schedule. So much for being caught up by Friday.

I have been on the phone tonight since I got home. First, my girlfriend from the Island called. That is always a long conversation. She is going to try and CHANGE her schedule so she can come out here in January for a few days. I told her she should try and make it for when we are planning to do the Belly Dancing at the Balkan. Cynthia is still trying to convince me to take lessons. I ask myself if this is something you may like.

I told her I wasn't too thrilled with the fact that you and I only get to see each other on Friday and Saturday nights and, besides the one cup of coffee, we have never actually seen each other in the day.. She told me, we should just enjoy each other. So, for now, I will be satisfied to call you my Friday/Saturday night special.

Norma, from Toronto, and I were almost like soul sisters back in the 80s and 90s, until she moved back East. We shared many of life's philosophies about love and spirituality. We also shared the music of Edith Piaf and others like her. When I had the children, we sort of drifted apart as she never did have children of her own. We all know how children have a tendency of producing CHANGE in a person.

She was telling me how she and Tim have been together twenty-two years now. I remember thinking when I was younger how I would never want to get married before I was thirty. I thought it would be too boring to be in a position to tell people that I was married to the same person for thirty years or more. At least now, I won't have to worry about that.

At one time, you told me you found an emotional solace in your music and this led me to think I have spent at least seven thousand dollars over the years on piano lessons for the children and neither one of them can sit down and actually play for me. Now I find myself with one of the top four keyboard players in the city and over the past two months you have only played for me once. I find this to be somewhat sad. No one wants to play for me.

Then Joanna phoned with her nightly call. Her advice to Gareth yesterday was if he planned to be held up in his room all day and all night over the holidays, he may as well move back to Saskatchewan. I still think she should get him a set of luggage for Christmas.

It is amazing. First, Norma tells me she misses me; next Joanna made her nightly call and said she supposed I wouldn't be coming over to visit, suggesting she also misses me. Earlier, Janis called to see if I could come over for a visit and she was disappointed when I said I wouldn't be able to, until Friday. Then, of course, there are my parents who were disappointed I couldn't stay more than ten minutes today and Julianna is always complaining we have so little time together anymore. The other day, Lily and Peter told me at lunch that they should have bought a house in Canmore and then they would have been closer to me. So everyone, it appears misses me......except you. I feel lucky though, that so many others do.

Miss Me?

Chapter 33

Thursday Morning

I had another late night because I helped Julianna with her homework. I didn't help all that much because she left it for the last minute as usual and I couldn't give her too much of my sympathy or time. Now she will miss her morning classes because she didn't get to bed until 4:00 or 5:00 this morning. I am not sure if she even did finish. I woke up at 4:00 and told her to go to bed and I would get her up around 10:00.

FREEDOM BREAKS WITH THE DAWN OF EACH DAY

This has been my motto for the last year and I was thinking of replacing it, but I haven't found a more suitable one. I feel I am free now and that is why it should be replaced. I love waking up in the morning with a new day, but then I always did. It is like the blank page I spoke of earlier. Cynthia is supposed to be finding me a new motto.

I have to go to work now. I still can't believe you haven't called. C'est la vie….again. Maybe you do have other women and are too busy trying to keep us all satisfied….to a certain degree….I think it is time you tossed me another bone….Thank God it is Thursday… one more day to go.

FREEDOM RULES!

Friday Morning

My mother couldn't wait until this morning for me to do her hair. She did it herself last night. Sometimes she is impatient. The only problem is she forgot to tell me and so I was there at 7:00, like we planned. I will see if I can get twelve hours worth of work done in the next eight. I have to pick up my clients at 8:20 as we are booked at the first house at 8:30. We are down to three houses now. They want to choose one of them today. This will be a nice Christmas present for me.

It was good to finally hear your voice last night. I thought you left town again. I have been busy at work and it seems like I haven't seen you for two weeks. I have one major dilemma. I need to figure this out by next week when I go into Calgary to get my Christmas gift from me to me. I need to find one of those love shops. I need to get myself a vibrator. The big dilemma is: do I buy a black one or a white one? I will answer this question as well. I will get a black one to start as I can always change colors later if needed. That may help shorten my week a bit or should we wind up missing a weekend I won't feel totally lost and won't have to go without sex.

PATIENCE RULES!

Friday Evening

I am toast! I have had the day from hell and have the privilege of telling you in person tonight so I will save it for then. Right now I am going to have a shower and a well- deserved nap. Oh, God it's 9:00. The nap will have to wait till next week.

See you…..later.

P.S. This wraps up the Christmas mail for you. I don't really want to end it that way. Let me finish by telling you. I am very, very happy we connected that night at Running Bull's. I cannot thank you enough for all the wonderful feelings you have given me in the last couple of months. You have been an unbelievable addition to the completion of what has actually been, in every way, a fantastic year of changes for me..

I do love you!
Irene

Chapter 34

Sent: December 23, 2006 1:26 A.M.
Subject: So sad you are sick

Well, it is 12:30 A.M. and this is not what I had in mind for to-night and neither did you. It was bound to happen sooner or later. I really hope you are feeling better tomorrow. I have a homemade remedy for the stomach flu. My mother makes it and it actually does work. She asks her sister in Germany to buy a mix of about thirty different herbs which the druggist mixes to my mother's request and then her sister ships it to my mom. Anyway, it can be effective.

When I finished the last letter, I said I would be able to tell you in person about my day from Hell. I guess I may as well write about it and then go to bed. Tomorrow night will be too busy, I hope, and in more WAYS than one.

I forgot to tell you on the phone I invited a couple of friends over for tomorrow night. I really hope you will be feeling better. If you are not, I will have to chase everyone out, which is what I basically told them anyway. It is too late for me to cancel. I told them I could only invite people who would know when it was time to leave, so they will not stay long anyway.

I want this day over, so I will hurry up. The day, of course, started with my mother's hair at 7:00, which she decided to do the night before. I had clients from 8:20 this morning until just after 10:00. Then I finished all my client Christmas mail and I decided to personalize all of them, which totalled fewer than eighty. I had to really think hard to try and remember where and when we met and what they were looking for. That was not easy, but I did manage fine. I actually received a number of replies already.

One young girl who works at the local hospital said she was happy to get my mail. She doesn't know too many people here yet and she wanted to know if we could have a coffee sometime. I will give her a call next week. Her boyfriend works in the oil rigs and he is seldom home. I think we may have something in common. I don't really know her because I only showed them property once for a couple of hours, but I always manage to find something to talk about.

This afternoon, I finally found the two hours I needed to do my power Christmas shopping and I have everything done, except for Julianna. I think I have that figured out now. I should be done by noon tomorrow. I picked up a bunch of Christmas bags because I knew I wouldn't have time for paper, tape and bows.

When I was done with that, I went grocery shopping and this is when things really went downhill. The parking lot was so full, I had to drive around and around for about ten minutes until I finally found a spot. I barely had a foot out of the door when Julianna called and asked me to pick her up at her girlfriend's and drive her to work. I asked her what time she worked and she said at 4:30.

The only problem was, it was exactly 4:30 and she was already late. I left my long sought- after parking spot to go pick her up and drop her at DQ. Then I drove back to the grocery store and wound up doing the same thing again, around and around. Finally, I got into the store and managed to get two aisles done, when my mother called to ask me if I was coming to do her hair for bingo. I totally forgot. I didn't tell her where I was and I said I would be there in five minutes.

I didn't even get a chance to turn around when I ran into clients whom I hadn't seen in two months. I spent a few minutes with them talking and setting up a meeting for next week. I took the stupid cart and gave it to the girl behind the service counter and told her I would be back to finish shortly and not to put anything away. The last thing I needed would be to start all over again. I couldn't believe I would have to do the parking lot a third time in the same afternoon.

When I finally finished with the groceries an hour and a half later, the bag guy asked me where my car was and I told him this was a good question. I told him I was called out twice and wound up having to park three different times that afternoon and, by now, I had no clue where it was. I started flipping the key thing pointing it in all

124

different directions, until the horn finally honked.

From there, with the groceries, I went to see Janis. My ninety-two year old wanted me to meet her sister and husband who were visiting from the coast. She is the one who phones me almost daily and I help her do her errands and things. So there I sat for an hour. She was happy I came over, but the next thing I knew she had fallen asleep. I spent most of the time talking to her sister and husband. They were very nice, but I was rushed and I actually had to wake up Janis to say goodbye.

I finally made it home around 7:00 and I had already made up my mind I was not going back tonight into the office to write an offer. Anyway, I am on floor duty in the afternoon tomorrow and it will have to wait until then.

My mother was in tears again tonight. She is still in so much pain from this surgery and as a result, she is depressed but she says she is only worried about me and that I am working too hard. It must be something in the air. Tomorrow should be far less hectic. I think I know why I enjoy writing so much. My jaw is sore from all the talking I have done this past week.

Another day done and I will go to bed now. I will say a little prayer that you will be better tomorrow. You know, I do have a number of guardian angels who look after me. We'll see if they are listening tonight.

If you are still too sick tomorrow, I am afraid I may lose it. I will spend the night with Hose Quervo and have my friends tuck me in. I will look forward to a call from you early in the day to let me know how you are feeling. I can't imagine going through another full day not knowing whether or not we will see each other tomorrow night.

Love
Irene…..now for my prayers.

Sent: December 23, 2006 8:37 A.M.
Subject: Finding Solace in your Pillow

Good morning? I wanted to catch you before you head into another busy day. It is 8:30 and I just woke up. I managed to find some solace last night by using your pillow, instead of mine, again.

I cheated yesterday when I changed the sheets in anticipation of your arrival. I didn't change the one pillow case because it still had the smell of your cologne on it. I do like it and it reminds me of you. It seems to me I have already written that this week. Who knows?

I put your pillow under my arm and ending at my nose, another up against my back and one big one for between my legs in hopes this will trick me into believing you are actually there. This is not something I thought of last night; rather, it is how I generally go to sleep, when you are not here. It is not quite the same as the real thing, but it does seem to help a little.

I must have known yesterday there was a chance you were going to be too ill to make it when I decided not to wash that pillow case. I will leave it as well today, just in case. Even if you are not totally up to snuff, can you please come anyway? We don't need to be wild about things. You can just lie there and I will rub your back. Maybe that will make you feel better.

I will wait for your call, with bated breath. I don't want to be shedding tears this Christmas.

Love
Irene

Chapter 35

Cephus did feel well enough the next evening and I wasn't disappointed a second night in a row. We did manage to get caught up and we had a bit of a feast. The following is the letter I set on top of the bundle of emails, wrapped in the beautiful musical bow I gave him for Christmas. I am almost certain he still has the bow, which is something a man generally does not keep.

Wishing you a Merry Christmas and may all your dreams come true in 2007!

I just want to thank you again for being a part of my life in 2006. I will start the New Year with new hopes and dreams for myself and a smile on my face, thanks to you.

The Ticketmaster gift certificate can be used for anything in Calgary from an opera at the Jubilee to a Flames game at the Saddledome. If I am lucky in 2007, I will be invited to join you and if not, you can always either go by yourself or ask one of your friends in Calgary to accom-

pany you. The other nice thing about this is if you are too busy to use it yourself, it is easy to re-gift. The socks are a joke and explained somewhere in the emails. As for the endurance drink, this is also a joke as you really don't need a drink like that. Maybe this is something you have been buying by the case.

If you feel even a little loved by all the writings and I hope you do, then I have accomplished something that is important to me. I love you and I hope the words are like music to your ears.

Irene

Christmas came and Cephus was not there for dinner. I was really hurt by this. I loved him very much; but why couldn't he be there on such an important day for me? Wasn't Christmas supposed to be a time for loved ones, friends and family? I have no idea where he spent the day and what he ate and with whom. The, "with whom" was the part that bothered me the most and it was slowly eating away at me. I was beginning to think that maybe he was still living with Lisa, the mother of his son.

It was hard for me not to picture the four of them sitting having a wonderful Christmas dinner together. The picture stayed with me all through Christmas. Not having an answer to the dinner invitation seemed to be so unnecessary. Why would he want to hurt me like that? The thoughts of him still living with her were not pleasant. Knowing a number of things about Caribbean men and their culture didn't help either. Needless to say, I shed a few tears over Christmas, but mostly I tried to stick with the "cheers" at Joanna's, so as not to get too depressed. I woke up on Boxing Day thinking, "Thank God. Christmas is over". Now I could maybe look forward to being with Cephus at some point, somewhere on New Year's Eve.

Part Seven
The Betrayal

Chapter 36

Sent: December 28, 2006 3:07 A.M.Subject: I will continue

I forget now where I was before Christmas. It has been so long. It wasn't very pleasant sleeping in the house alone last night. I can't imagine when Julianna finishes school and leaves home and Danny and I live by ourselves in this big house. I will definitely have to get it ready to sell.

The only question is if I will get a mortgage on my own, being out of the workforce for nine years and not having an income to speak of. I stopped working the Bed and Breakfast two years ago and last year my income was only $3000.00. Somehow I don't think they will look favourably at that number and they may just ignore assets.

My mother has been talking about them moving into the lodge, but I don't want them to do that. For years now, we have been talking about us living together under one roof, when they couldn't look after themselves anymore. We planned that they would live on the main level and I would live in a separate suite above.

I forgot to tell you that I did write that nice letter for Joanna this Christmas and I stuck it in with her gift. It has probably been a very long time since someone told her how valuable a person she is. I was right. She said she cried twice on Christmas morning, thinking of all the things I wrote in the letter. The truly wonderful thing was that everything I wrote was actually true. I think this is what I am meant to give her—either the strength to stick it out with Gareth or the strength to get rid of him and, of course, the strength then to carry on. It really hurts me that Gareth hardly ever has a kind word for her and that was the real reason for the letter in the first place and the timing of it.

I have really screwed up my day today. I am with the Brits this afternoon as they fly home tomorrow. They saw nine places yesterday and want to see three of them again and then they will decide. It will take all afternoon to look at these and then write the offer. It is doubtful we will be finished today. Then we will have to continue by fax or email which is less than ideal because of the time difference.

I totally forgot yesterday that I had told Lily and Peter we would meet today for lunch. I was supposed to run up to Banff to meet them and I had to cancel at the last minute. This is not nice. Maybe we can have dinner here in Canmore tonight and we can take care of the rest of our business then. I am also in the middle of the other offer, with the people from Toronto. That offer is only open until 9:00 tonight. It's a good thing I've always been good at multitasking. This is something I really perfected in my furniture store days.

I always thrived on this level of activity. If it is quiet, I don't function as well and it seems I get nothing done; but if it is busy, I can generally do the work of two or three in a day.

Now the sun is up and I told the Brits today's sky would be blue and it is. This will probably mean they will wind up buying the most expensive property I showed them yesterday. It overlooks the whole Valley with a million dollar view, which will look worth a million more with blue skies. I don't think they will diddle too much with the price, if the color of the sky is right. It really is magnificent and to top things off, it is a great price.

I also forgot to mention my cousin from the Foothills invited the kids and me for New Year's and to stay overnight. I know the kids would love his massive indoor pool. I have already told Cynthia I would come to hers, but I could CHANGE my mind. I am certain you will be playing somewhere in Calgary that night. You will be too busy to spend time with me, so I may as well spend the evening with my friends.

I have to jump into the shower now. I am glad I won't have to sleep in the house alone again tonight. At least I hope someone will be here. It was nice to see you loosen up a bit the other night. I guess you feel more comfortable without the children in the house. Another year and they will be gone. A few years ago, I was crying, thinking about the empty nest syndrome. I wonder what it will really be like once they are gone.

I will just have to find myself some roommates like when I was young. Throughout my marriage, we always had the house full of people. We had the live-in nannies for six years and all those Japanese, German and Belgium exchange students. Then there were all those hockey kids and Rotary Club GSI groups or whatever they were called. I have told Julianna that when she needs roommates, she should pick the guys over the girls as they tend to be much cleaner.

See you later

Love
Irene

P.S. Everyone loves my treble clef pendant, especially me.

Chapter 37

Sent: December 30, 2006 2:59 A.M.
Subject: Sleepless in Canmore

I just wanted to quickly thank you for your call at midnight, telling me you weren't coming over tonight. After I hung up the phone, I wondered why my initial response was so pleasant. Not two minutes passed and my phone rang again and it was Joanna. She has gotten into the habit, the past three weeks, of phoning me at midnight to see if you are going to make it or not that night. I wonder if she is concerned about me. I told her you just called and cancelled and I would be right over, as that I had just spent an hour getting all guzzied up for you. I thought I may as well see someone.

What you possibly don't realize is, I purposely had a nap tonight so I would be wide awake after midnight when you came. I even had Joanna give me a wake up call at 10:00 tonight so I could get ready.

Speaking of which, women do take some time to get ready, you know. I am certain you knew this morning, or at least at some point during the course of the day, that you were not going to stay the night in Canmore. Your plans for the day did not materialize at midnight tonight. Why wouldn't you tell me earlier? Did you lose my phone number? Why would you wait until midnight? I could have saved showering a second time today, doing my hair a second time today and doing my makeup a second time today. Now, because of this stupid nap I had tonight, I can't sleep anymore. It is 1:45 A.M. and I am still wide awake and look what I am doing now............

Somewhere in that mass of emails, I thought I wrote something about the goose and the gander and I am not into playing....games at my age and neither should you. What I would like for you to do is to think of what it would feel like if you were expecting to see me some evening and instead my phone would go to message.

I do have a life and I do like to plan my Friday and Saturday nights for networking. In case you are wondering, this is a term for seeking out prospective clients. Those are the two key nights when people are out. What I have found myself doing the last number of weeks is planning them so I can rush home and wait for your call, which can be anywhere from 10:30 P.M. to 1:30 A.M. I think you are somehow forgetting something here. I am under the impression I need to be home by about 9:00 P.M., in order to freshen up for you, just in case.

I mentioned to you before I was invited to my cousin's in Calgary for New Year's and you haven't mentioned a word about what you have planned or your schedule. I was actually planning on being in the city for New Year's, thinking this is where you would be and there may be a chance of seeing you for even a brief time. I found out from my mother tonight you are actually booked for Benny's. I can't believe you couldn't tell me you were actually playing New Year's out here and I had to hear it first from my mother who got it from the newspaper.

After all of this confusion, I told her I would be happy just to stay at home. All you ever told me about New Year's was you MAY be playing out here. I never pressed you for a definitive answer and maybe that was my only mistake. It would be nice if you could tell me your plans and your schedule in advance so I don't need to CHANGE my plans.

Now, don't get this whole email wrong. I am not really upset. I only want you to consider it as me, informing you about how I feel, before I do get upset. Leaving me in the dark until the midnight hour is not a kind thing to do to me……. to anyone.

There are three question marks on this email and they don't require an answer as I did promise you I would not ask anymore this year. I would like it, if you have time during the course of the year, that you either give me a call or send me an email and let me know if you plan on staying tomorrow and Sunday night. This way, I can plan the rest of my year.

Thank you for your kind consideration, regarding this matter.

Sleepless in Canmore

Now the New Year's Eve plan for me was to go to Cynthia's party. I would ask Cephus to pick me up there when he would call that night and after they had finished playing. The big mistake I made this evening was thinking that the music would stop no later than 12:30 A.M. and then everyone would go home. I'd not attended very many New Year's Eve dos, outside of someone's home and I never even thought of them having to play any later than that. I enjoyed the evening at Cynthia's, but I found that I was checking my watch far too often. It was not in the countdown to the New Year, but in the countdown to when I would be with Cephus.

Cephus called at about 1:20 A.M. and said he would only be about twenty minutes. I was tired of waiting by this time and I had Stewart and Diane drive me home. I couldn't wait to get into the door to shed my first tears of the New Year. Once inside, I made sure to have another drink, to try and cheer me up, but it didn't. I remembered all those New Year's Eves when I sat by myself, before I was married, crying and watching that stupid ball drop in New York. How could I have wound up alone here again on this night?

I went to bed and fell asleep, still waiting. He finally arrived at about 3:00 and he woke me up as if nothing was wrong. I was finished. I hadn't seen him all week and by the time he arrived, I was already asleep, then he would spend a couple of hours together with me in the morning and then he would be gone again for another week. The constant anticipation of his arrivals and the sadness associated with the quick departures were too much to take anymore.

The next morning I was invited to brunch at Joanna's and Cephus said he couldn't attend. Why, I didn't know. His standard answer was that he had a lot to do and he was busy. By now my suspicion was solid that he had to get back to his wife and children. I couldn't imagine he had a gig on New Year's Day as everyone would be home nursing their hangovers, similar to me. I told him he should drop me off at Joanna's and when I turned to say goodbye, I fought back the tears. I knew in my mind I needed to get away from him, before he had the chance to turn me into a real basket case. I could barely look him in the eye because I was afraid I would really break down and I would not be able to stop the tears.

Chapter 38

Sent: January 2, 2007 7:22 A.M.
Subject: The Midnight Train

I am sure you must be scratching your head, wondering what was going on in my head yesterday morning. It is time for this relationship to move out of my bedroom and into the daylight hours, if it is going to move ahead.

I woke up yesterday morning thinking about all that waiting and anticipation of your arrival and there you were leaving again. I really felt like some hooker and the only thing missing was the cash on the nightstand. I am trying to get out of town this weekend as I really need a break from the last two and one half months of our late night rendezvous in my bedroom. It is definitely time for the scenery to change.

Please don't phone me this Friday or Saturday in case I don't get a ticket on that midnight train out of here and I may not have the strength not to answer your call. You can call me when you are ready to meet me in the daytime for coffee and then we can talk.

The Hooker on Main Street

Sent: January 3, 2007 11:01 A.M.
Subject: Re: The Midnight Train

It was nice to hear from you for I was puzzled about Monday morning, the first day of the New Year. So you have cleared that up in my head for me, thanks.

At least you heard something that I said that morning as I was dropping you off at Joanna's and that was my suggestion that I not call you after midnight. We are on the same page with that so I won't call you after midnight. You don't have to leave your hometown or family for fear that I'm going to invade your space, seduce you and turn you into a "hooker" or make you feel like one.

Speaking of "hooker" where did that come from? When did I force my way into your bedroom and make you this way? My biggest question is why would someone get out of an eighteen year marriage and then choose to have the next relationship with some "old fart" that makes her miserable and downgraded like "the hooker on Main Street"?

I don't need an answer for that really. It doesn't make me feel any better. Hope your business is doing great.

Luv
Larry

Sent: January 3, 2007 1:59 P.M.
Subject: Where it comes from?

So if you can't and won't call me after midnight, I suppose I will never hear from you again, which is exactly my point. If I were in your shoes, I would have hustled my buns out to Canmore to take the "old girl" for a cup of coffee and if I didn't have the time, I would have made the time.

Cephus, I have been suggesting for a long time that we do something in the daytime, regardless of how brief and these were not just hints, as the emails were full of suggestions. There isn't a woman on earth I know who would be content just to see "her guy" at night and never in the day. You seem to be okay with this; though, you haven't said a word or made a move to spend even a couple of hours with me during the course of a day, any day, doing whatever, other than in my bedroom. This is where it comes from.

Unfortunately, it hit me like a ton of bricks on New Year's Day, when you left so quickly. I waited until 3:00 A.M. for you and then there you were, leaving again. That was when everything came crashing down and I started to feel like this hooker. You really don't ever want to see me in the daylight; otherwise, you would have made some attempt. You can't use your age as an excuse and, on the contrary, with all this wisdom you have accumulated throughout your lifetime, you should know what women need and how they want to be treated. You are the one who keeps telling me how much you understand women and what they are feeling.

You and I never connecting in the daytime makes me think, you either don't want to be seen with me in public or maybe you just think I look better in the dark. I don't know. It seems to me that I wrote that once before as well. After all, Cephus, it has been two and a half months and it is not like we just started seeing each other.

I'm at work and have to go now. It is getting crowded around here and I don't want to start crying. Talk to me soon.

Love you still
Irene

Sent: January 3, 2007 3:31 P.M.
Subject: Irene's P.S.

I forgot to tell you my New Year's resolution. It is to not receive a midnight call from you again until we have had a legitimate daytime date. What do you think about that? Now, this is a question for you and I would really like an answer to this one. After all, it is a New Year.

Forever Waiting.........and getting better at it.

Chapter 39

Sent: January 4, 2007 9:01 A.M.
Subject: In Simpler Terms

I have done my own arithmetic and it is the eighty-second day of this relationship and I am still waiting for you to ask me out. There comes a point when a woman has to ask herself if this guy really likes her or is he just after the sex. Surely in eighty-two days he would have found the time to see her before midnight on one of those days. If you can't understand this, then maybe you should consult Allison and she can explain it to you. I don't know too many women who would wait that long, other than Jane in Banff or someone like that.

You see, your age and the fact that you are a musician really has nothing to do with it. I don't think you really like me well enough to see me or get to know me, other than in the bedroom. I can't believe I actually had a twinge of jealousy thinking about the clerks at Mappin's Jewellery, where you bought my pendent and the clerks at Long & McQuade Music Store who, and not me, have seen you and know you in the daytime. So where is the justice and fair treatment in this?

Yes, I'm in pain and suffering and this must make you happy because you refuse to do anything about it. I will just have to get over it.

Simple Irene

Cephus ignored my request about not calling. I was over at Joanna's on Thursday night and as he was passing by Canmore, he called on his way to play Buffalo's. It was good to hear his voice again, but I was still very angry with him and adamant about not seeing him again in the dark. I was finally beginning to see and understand what

Taurus was all about and the meaning of what I read in the beginning of the relationship. Taurus turn out to be notorious for putting their loved ones on a shelf, only to take them down and occasionally dust them. Sent: January 5, 2007 7:37 A.M.

Subject: Change Equation

I think I misunderstood you last night. Is this what you insinuated.......?

Seeing me in the daytime = CHANGE

Are you telling me you have not been with a woman in the daytime since your last serious relationship in 2003? You really should come out of the dark! If not, you should ask Jane out for one of your after midnight rendezvous. This is the way the equation should read.

Seeing me in the daytime = NO CHANGE

I can't believe a simple cup of coffee can create such a debate! After all, it is not like I am asking you to go climb a mountain with me or to go skiing. I'll be turning my phone off tonight and unfortunately I will need to have it on during the day tomorrow. Please don't call then. No, I didn't get a ticket out of here so I will turn off my phone again tomorrow evening. The weekend is here and I have booked myself to work all day, each day and I have also made sure I will be kept busy both nights until at least 1:00 A.M. This way I will not have to suffer through the pain of missing you alone. Come to think of it, there are many people who love me in the DAY and in the NIGHT. You are just not one of them.

Hope to talk to you next week.

Love and Miss You
Irene

P.S. I have decided to replace you with the gym, which is a much healthier choice for me right now. I will definitely need to get into Calgary next week and look for that love shop. I will not be able to make it through a second weekend without and, no, I am not changing the color.

Chapter 40

We had reached a crucial point in our relationship and as our horns locked, I thought it was over. We were still communicating, but we certainly weren't getting anywhere fast. I really felt I would have to be the one to put an end to all this misery that I was going through. It didn't appear he was going to make the move and I felt it would be left up to me. He did tell me once it would take a great deal of effort for him to walk away from a relationship.

I was in this same place before with someone else early in my life. I was dating an undercover narcotics' member of the R.C.M.P. for a number of years and the relationship wasn't going anywhere for either of us. I ended it peacefully, by telling him not to call me anymore. Maybe the end to this one would be similar.

What I didn't realize was that I was in a dangerous position with my present frame of mind. In my head I went back to the days in my early thirties and when I was dating David and all those crazy years together with him. It was in this relationship I discovered, or so I thought, the only way to drive a man out of a woman's head was to hop into bed with another. It didn't work back then, but it didn't prevent me from trying. I found myself dating, first two, and then three men at the same time, for what seemed like quite awhile. The second wound up killing himself, not because of me, and the third one, I married.

Friday night came and I spent the evening with Joanna, talking about Cephus until she must have been sick of it. She didn't say anything, but just listened and let me ramble. The next night I told my parents that I needed to get out and that I would go with them to Banff and Running Bull's. I hadn't gone out, other than to Joanna's, since October and when Cephus and I had reconnected that night.

On January 6th, I spent the evening talking and dancing with my father and trying to be happy and not think about Cephus, but it wasn't working. The place was not very busy for a Saturday night and, in a way, I was glad. I wasn't really in the mood for having a good time. I reached a point, later in the evening, when I asked myself why I felt I couldn't do anything, except think of him. This really upset me. How could I let someone control me and my emotions like that? Why did I feel it necessary to waste all this time and energy on a man who didn't really love me?

Then this thirty-something year old British med student asked me to dance. That is when I finally cut loose and tried to drown Cephus out of my thoughts. The Brit and I wound up in a cab together, heading for Canmore and, a couple of hours later, he left the same way.

Now if this wasn't enough to end a relationship, then nothing would. I found I was asking myself: "could I ever go back to Cephus after this night?" I loved him so much and didn't really want the relationship to end. If I didn't want it to end, then why was I trying so hard? According to some clinical study on divorced couples, January 7th seemed to be the most prominent day of the year for couples to actually separate. I wonder if it was mere coincidence the cab ride occurred in the wee hours of the 7th.

By Tuesday, I discovered I failed in my attempt to end the relationship with Cephus. I really missed him. Maybe the pain of the relationship and the thoughts that he was possibly still living with a woman, were not so bad after all. Now I would only need to add the pain of guilt on top of everything else I had to deal with. Besides, the begging for forgiveness already began with my first email, in the "I am Sorry" and the "I promise to be good".

Chapter 41

Sent: January 9, 2007 7:12 A.M.
Subject: I am Sorry

I guess you didn't consult Allison last week, but I decided to ask Julianna. Sometimes it helps to ask someone who may have a different perspective on things and the young often have fresher ideas and more realistic expectations than us older people.

Julianna gave me a big lecture last night on how I owe you an apology and she did manage to convince me for the most part. I am very sorry! She says I push too hard and my New Year's resolution should be broken and it is meant to be. She says I expected too much from you and too quickly. She said my resolution was more like an ultimatum and I guess it's true. She continued to tell me no one likes ultimatums and I know she is right. I am confused though, as I really didn't look at it that way. All I could think of was you didn't like me well enough to see me in the day, for whatever reason. Julianna added something about my tunnel vision. I also received an email from my sister and, out of the blue, she said I should watch I don't get too cocky and she wasn't even talking about you. So I have been receiving nothing but lectures this past week.

I did need this last weekend without you, to try and figure out some things. I don't think it helped much, as I am still very confused. The one thing I do know for certain is the weekend turned out to be a very long one for me. Work was good and the rest was horrible. My great plan of being so occupied backfired and I was the only one heartbroken by it.

I miss you way too much! Is there anyway you and I can get together again to talk about things or are you so pissed off now, you never want to see me again? Can you please call so we can talk? I am trying to set up an appointment with my lawyer in Calgary for either Thursday or Friday. Could we meet for coffee then or on the weekend when you are out here? I promise I will be good.

I am at the staff meeting this morning, but will have my phone on after that. My number hasn't changed.

Love and miss you
Irene

By Tuesday night I had shared with Julianna and Joanna my secret of the previous weekend.. I tried all of the following Sunday not to feel guilty about what had happened, but in my heart I felt sick about it. In my mind, the brief encounter should have made me recognize that my relationship with Cephus was actually over and that I would get on with my life and be in charge again. Somehow, I thought miraculously, I would stop thinking about him and missing him but it didn't work. I was left to deal with all this guilt. I shared what happened that night in hopes of diminishing the real importance of it and that didn't work either. I even tried bragging about it. Here I was, fifty-three years old and still able to seduce a thirty year old. I was disgusted with myself and my lifelong attempt at mentoring Mother T. Had my whole life been a lie?

Julianna and Joanna both told me, whatever I did, I should not tell Cephus what had happened and I should forget it and carry on with the relationship. How could I keep such a secret though, from someone I loved so much? I was always open and honest and how could I change now and keep this from him? I thought of all those years of being married and never even having thoughts of being unfaithful. How could I stop myself from feeling cheap and dirty?

Sent: January 10, 2007 11:51 A.M.
Subject: Mother Teresa

I understand myself better today with the help of Joanna, Julianna and everyone else who has been mad at me for the last week, including you. This is the first time since I was twenty-six that I have put myself ahead of everyone else in my life and it is new to me. It has altered my normal behaviour, whatever that is. I don't know anymore. I went through so many changes this past year and I find myself in a place where I never expected to be in my life, and divorced.

I started the store when I was so young and since that time I have put all my needs and wants on a back burner. My staff and the business were always more important than anything I needed. They always came first when it came time for payday and days off and I was always dead last.

Then I got married and had children and this is when I fell even further behind in the scheme of things. Now I was dead last at work and at home. By this time I had about six or seven people working for me in the store, two children, a live-in nanny and, of course, a husband, not to mention my parents. At the height of all this, in the early 90s, I worked at least eighty hours per week between the store and home. This is why I have to laugh when people today try and suggest that if I don't slow down, I will burn myself out.

I had all these people I was responsible for, not only their livelihoods, but their emotional needs as well. Often I felt like I was nothing more than a glorified babysitter with a staff, with whom I had to constantly intervene when personalities clashed. At home, I had the same job description. Even the dog's needs came before mine, as I also looked after him.

The way I see it, I don't have as much baggage, as you call it, from a failed marriage as I do from being overworked all those years and never having time for myself. All year I've been trying to spoil myself by not only with making time for myself, but also through buying anything I wanted. I agree this is not right and I know it won't last. Everyone is complaining, especially the children and my parents. God knows how they complain about the little time that I spend with them these days.

You should have heard them when I told them that I had spent three thousand dollars on clothes in one evening's shopping spree. They know I've spent a great deal and are wondering where my head is at, but it is my money and not theirs. Besides, nothing I had fit me anymore. It was definitely needed and I could also justify my spending habits of the year with the fact that I went through almost eighteen years of marriage with hardly ever buying anything new for myself. I guess you might say I tried hard to buy the eighteen years' worth and I am still behind.

What I think has happened to us, is I have this inner urge to put you behind me, along with everyone else in my life right now. This is the problem I have to rectify and seeing it now, at least allows me the opportunity to correct it.

I had my cards read this week and they say this new attitude of mine, me first, has made me into my own worst enemy. I guess they were right and I had better get to work fixing myself. The big joke is I thought I was perfect for the most part.

To start this change in me, I should ask you if there is anything I can do for you, just let me know. Maybe I can get back to being Mother Teresa again.

Mother T.

Chapter 42

Cephus called in the evening and told me he would come out to see me on Thursday, before playing Buffalo's. I was surprised by his call and his efforts to try to take my feelings into consideration. I began to see hope for the relationship after all, in spite of my indiscretion and guilt.

Earlier in the week, I had made arrangements to meet Lily and Peter at Buffalo's that night for dinner. Cephus was going to join us for a bit and we would hear him play. I hadn't heard him since Benny's and the night of my birthday party and our first fight. I was nervous again and excited at the same time. I was looking forward to spending some time with him and my friends.

The three of us sat on the restaurant side of Buffalo's and ordered our meal. Cephus was nowhere in sight until he came up from behind and gave me a peck on the cheek. He sat down with us for what amounted to only about twenty minutes. I felt proud we were together as a couple in public, even if the rest of the place didn't know it. I could tell by the look on his face he was also happy I was there.

I began to recognize the look of love in his eyes and in his gestures. I often thought this sixty-three year old took on the facial expressions of a child when he was happy. I had seen the look in him before, as I did again this night. I saw it the time we met in Calgary for the cup of coffee in the day. He was excited to the point of appearing to float, much like a child going to see the circus for the first time. Many times in bed, it seemed he couldn't snuggle up close enough and it was like he wanted to curl up under my skin. I loved it because it was where I wanted to be.

Lily and Peter and I moved into the lounge area after our dinner and Chuck came over, during the course of a song, and gave me a hug. I was accustomed to this, as this was his routine and it became a part of who he was on stage. In all the times I listened to Cephus play at Benny's, I never once heard him sing by himself without Chuck. The three of us were involved in conversation and, all of a sudden, I stopped to look and listen. It was a Bob Marley tune I had never heard before, but I recognized the reggae beat. I was shocked to see Cephus was singing and not Chuck. The name of the tune was "Waiting". I turned to Lily and Peter and told them I was certain he was singing it for me and I felt special. I remembered him telling me he waited three years for me. I asked him later if he had played and sang the song for me and all he did was change the subject and he kept his heart closed.

Sent: January 14, 2007 9:48 A.M.
Subject: Good Morning…..Lover

I am so happy you turned out to be a lover and not a fighter and I had a wonderful day yesterday as a result. It appears I am back to being, calm, relaxed and productive. I will try not to push you so hard in the future, which tends to screw both of us up.

The only thing I didn't get done yesterday was to spend some time with my parents. I haven't seen them much this past week at all and they are not happy as a result. I will try to go over this morning, after the laundry and before I go to work. .

Things are looking up at home as Julianna took it upon herself to clean the bird's cage. Peaches is very happy now. We still didn't get to watch that movie together because she had a friend over to study last night. She is happy you are back on the scene and prefers that I am calm.

I phoned my British clients yesterday and she will be getting in touch with her husband, who is in Indonesia right now. They will finally decide on which property they will buy. The other one that they had had the offer on, turned into a bidding war with another couple and they lost. They will have to beef up their offer considerably or I don't think they will get this one either. I hope she will come around as it really has their name on it and they love it.

My American client leaves today and wants to do the offer via email from home. He is still debating too much on which one to buy. He is one of those analytical types and a recent graduate, with a master's in business. He spent all of last week analysing the financial statements of three different hotel vacation rental properties that I had given him. He is also debating whether or not to put the property in his girlfriend's name. I don't think their relationship is strong enough and this is his dilemma. I told him to put it in his name and be done with it.

The open house in Banff turned out to be a lucrative one after all. Everyone had told me it would be a waste of my time, as no realtors do open houses in Banff. I wasn't there thirty minutes and the first of only two couples walked in. Guess who the first were. A man, black as night from Burkina Faso, with his girlfriend, and you thought there were no other black people in the Valley besides Chuck. It must have been the good luck charm you gave me for Christmas because I am showing them one other property on Monday and then they will decide. I have referred them to a mortgage broker for Monday morning and I am sure they will be fine.

He moved from Montreal where he had lived for ten years and his girlfriend has only been in Canada one year. It would be amazing if they bought this condo, as it is right next door to the one I sold Lily and Peter. Lily is originally from Montreal and Peter is from Luxembourg; they only speak French when they are alone. The main language in Burkina Faso happens to be French as well. I think they would get along well as neighbours. The four of them seem to be intellectual and worldly. The other thing that they have in common is they are all relatively new immigrants and new to being in business for themselves. Lily and Peter met at university in England and moved to Luxembourg after they were married. They lived there for fifteen years and she actually gave up her Canadian Citizenship for the Luxembourg one.

Enough of that! I will finish this by telling you the day was filled with warm and pleasant thoughts of you. I passed the day feeling like you were still inside me, which I always find amazing. The feeling was so strong I had one of those mini orgasms on the drive home from Banff, just thinking about you. I landed back in Canmore, with a smile on my face and content.

I never did get a chance to thank you for coming up early on Thursday. I really do appreciate your efforts. I know you don't believe in horoscopes, but my mother keeps cutting them out for me. Last week mine was really bad. It said if I had all the answers, why was no one asking me for advice? It said I should learn a thing or two from others this week. That is why I spent so much time listening to everyone lecture me about our relationship. Yours, on the other hand, said that something that seemed insurmountable was actually much easier to scale and you would reach even greater heights. I hope you have.

This week your horoscope stated that you have to take responsibility for your actions, even if those actions aren't the most honourable and you will redeem yourself. You definitely found redemption in my eyes, by showing up here so early on Thursday before Buffalo's.

This week my horoscope was better and it stated that my elegant way was like a breath of fresh air and that while others were full of pomp and circumstance, I would quietly make a place for myself in this world. I am glad everyone brought me back to earth last week with their lectures.

I hope you have a good day today and I wonder if I will be able to extend yesterday's warm thoughts of you into today. That would be nice, but I am always worried people can read my mind and tell by the expression on my face about what I am really thinking. I spent many years talking to myself in front of the stove. I am always worried I will moan out loud when I have those little orgasms and then they will really know. It isn't funny, as I have caught myself doing just that and even at work. Lucky for me no one was there, I hope.

Love
Irene

I didn't tell Cephus that his horoscope fit me better than it did him and it was me who needed redemption. My sin was far greater than anything he did wrong in this relationship. I was thankful he was

152

emotionally much stronger than I was and he generally appeared calm and balanced. Nothing seemed to ruffle his feathers. I saw in him all that impressed me so much, through my years of travel and my impressions of the culture of island people. I was thankful, when we were together that I was able to draw on this energy of his and find peace within myself. Unfortunately, the energy would ultimately dissipate a couple of days after he left and I was, once again, left to deal with my own emotions and thoughts.

Four days passed without hearing a word from him and I went from this emotional calm of Sunday to nothing, but chaotic turmoil by Thursday. The emotional roller coaster I was on, was really beginning to wear me down and I was about to snap.

Chapter 43

Sent: January 18, 2007 12:03 A.M.
Subject: Gone but not forgotten?

Gone but not forgotten.........or just gone and forgotten?

Love
???????

I arranged to meet Lily and Peter in Banff for dinner again and then we planned to head over to Buffalo's. I met up with them at Maggie's. While we were sitting there, I thought I would give Cephus a call to see if he could join us. He had called, which became routine for us, to let me know he had arrived in the Valley.. I was mistakenly under the impression it shouldn't take more than a half hour to set up. I gave him a call back and asked if he would have a half hour to spare and be with us. He told me he would try to make it. When I hung up the phone, I told Lily and Peter he was going to join us and when he didn't show I was embarrassed, upset and feeling even more uncomfortable than I had felt when I had started out in the evening. I assumed he didn't want to be with me and, therefore, he could maintain this aloof attitude with our relationship.

When we walked into Buffalo's, we sat in the corner and more or less out of sight, but I was certain he noticed us come in. During the course of the evening, he again played and sang the Marley tune. The whole night passed without his acknowledgement of my existence and this made me uncomfortable. I did, however, get my usual hug from Chuck and that made me feel even worse.

I went home, after two glasses of wine at the club, feeling totally miserable and alone and with the burning question in my mind about whether or not he really cared about me. When I arrived home, I immediately put on the Bob Marley CD. Danny had burned it for me over the previous weekend and since then I played it over and over again. I also printed out the words so I could sing along. I freshened up, which was now my habit and I poured myself a glass of vodka to soothe the pain in my chest. By the time Cephus arrived at 2:00 A.M., I was no longer sober and I was barely awake.

I acted as though everything was fine, but it wasn't. I could be just as aloof about the relationship as he could be and I became cold and uncaring. True to human nature, when self preservation kicked in, I began to erect my own brick wall. My defence mechanism, for all this hurt, was sarcasm and I pretended that I didn't care.

The drink loosened my tongue enough by then and I began to tell him stories of my previous sexual escapades. After all, I listened to a lifetime of his. I told him of one in particular, I had with I was a thirty year old. When he questioned me the next morning about when this fling had happened in my life, I lied to him and said it was months earlier. He didn't question me further, but he no sooner left and I felt fifty times worse for having lied to him.

He wasn't on the highway more than ten minutes, when I called him on his cell and told him that I had lied and the affair actually happened the weekend we didn't see each other. I talked for awhile, trying to explain, but the news left him speechless. All he could say was that he thought something didn't add up.

Chapter 44

Sent: January 20, 2007 7:45 A.M.
Subject: Need to talk

Hello

I really need to speak with you and preferably today if we can. The only problem is I would rather do it in person instead of email or on the phone. Is this possible?

Irene

There was no response from Cephus. I think I listened to the Marley tune about a hundred times more since Friday and I knew the words by heart now and no longer needed the sheet. What was worse, I felt justified in my actions and what I did January 6th. I endured so much pain since December and before Christmas. What I didn't understand, was Cephus's feelings and maybe this is why I kept pressing on.

It is difficult to let go of things in life and not worry about the necessity to find answers to the "whys". Maybe this is the reason I was always reluctant to find out details about specific events and I tended to hesitate to ask too many questions. I would accept whatever a person was willing to tell me. I knew the "why", actually had the potential of sometimes pushing us over the edge. The "why" in this relationship was driving me crazy and what if the answer was that he is married?

I was always eager and ready to answer any and all of the questions that my children ever put to me; the standard response of most parents was, "Because, I say so". This was something that always annoyed me. Parents would refuse to take the time to answer their child's questions, leaving them to think that they were not worthy of proper answers and then the parents wondered "why" they couldn't communicate with their children when they were in their teens. Thinking of all my unanswered questions should have been enough to drive anyone mad.

The waiting, for me was now finally over, along with the relationship and I no longer needed to wait for an answer to any of the questions that may never have come anyway.

Sent: January 20, 2007 10:10 A.M.
Subject: Gone but not forgotten

On Thursday night, when Lily, Peter and I went out for dinner, I assumed because it was early, you would have time to stop by for a half hour and join us. When you didn't show up, I felt like such a fool again. There I was, with that unbearable waiting, waiting, and waiting.

I had one of the better weekends with you, possibly because of the eleven days' break from each other. Everything I wrote in the Sunday email was true. If you remember, when you phoned me on Monday, you said you were trying to find time to come out here during the day sometime this week. I was excited as I would finally be able to see you out here in the day and my waiting would finally come to an end. Monday to Wednesday was not bad as I put in at least thirty-five hours of work in those three days and hardly had time to think about you.

By Thursday, you still hadn't phoned, not even a one minute call to tell me you couldn't find the time. This is not good. You need to face it, Cephus; if this is the way you treat all of your relationships, it is no wonder you are generally not in one. You don't have time for one and you refuse to make the time. This would mean you don't really want one in the first place.

The hooker email was not far from the truth. When we didn't see each other for the eleven days, I fell into bed with the thirty year old, not for the sex, but to disgust myself and force an end to the relationship. I wanted to drive you out of my heart. Well, it didn't work, other than the part of being disgusted and ashamed with my behaviour and, instead of driving you out of my mind, I let you in deeper. I am so very sorry for cheating on you and I do hope you will forgive me for that. I also know the reason why I found it imperative to tell you what I did and not keep it a dark secret.

It turned out not to be a healthy relationship for me since December and, if I didn't end it now, I could wind up making myself very sick. On Thursday night I had two glasses of wine in Banff and when I came home, I questioned whether I should go to sleep for a couple of hours or wait as usual. Sleep was what I really wanted and I got into my pyjamas. Lying there in bed, I felt cheap waiting for you dressed like that and so I whipped out of bed and got dressed again. I put on my Marley tunes and decided to try and perk up by having a couple of shots of vodka. I did not want to be sad and depressed when you got there. What I also realized that night, was this became somewhat of a routine with me to get ready for you and to have a few drinks to keep me awake; last summer with my friends I had stayed up all night dancing, only three or four times over the three month period.

That night was the straw that broke the camel's back. I was so tired from having such a busy week and there I was drinking and waiting, instead of sleeping, which I so desperately wanted to do. I cannot do this anymore and it needs to end right now. I need a daytime relationship, a normal daytime relationship.

In my mind, there has been nothing normal about us. Three months of not ever going out with you and seeing you in the day, is not normal and it is bringing out some pretty crazy and abnormal behaviour in me and it needs to stop.

You said yesterday. I was all over the map the night before. Well, I have good news for you. I am not all over the map other than this bad side of me you seem to have brought out. I told you yesterday, during the day, I am very busy, but always calm and generally collected, NEVER MOODY and always upbeat and full of happy energy. I don't think you have ever seen this side of me as YOU have chosen never to see me in the day.

My friends and family do know this day person and scratch their heads wondering why the hell I am waiting for you. Many cannot understand why they have never met you or why they have never seen us together as a couple. They find this not normal either and keep telling me I deserve more and should get on with it.

You can't really blame this on the fact that you're a musician. You only need to look around to see many other musicians who are in lasting or long term relationships and they do exist in the light as well as in the dark. It is only you and I who don't have that. For relationships to continue to grow, they cannot be kept in a bed in a dark room, where YOU have put ours. It needs air and light to grow, which ours does not have. You should not be surprised, when the relationship dies.

I do love you and I am very sad to have to end it. I would like to say we can be friends, but I find it highly unlikely this could work either, as friends see each other in the daytime as well. You find it impossible to fit that into your schedule. Maybe we could be email buddies, but then you don't really like to write all that much either and you don't have the time.

Forget all that nonsense of my pushing you too hard and giving you ultimatums. You have had more than enough time to treat me with respect rather than showing up at my house after midnight all the time. Is it any wonder I wound up in the sack with the other guy? You have made me feel cheap now and I know I really am r not. For this, you owe me an apology, because it could have been very easy for you to have fit in a couple of hours with me in the daytime over all these months. You and I both have to stop kidding ourselves about your busy schedule, bullshit! You just chose not to.

Tell me you didn't feel wanted and loved by all those emails in which I poured my heart and soul out to you. I opened my heart and let you in and, in return for this kindness, you made me feel cheap. You have been playing this waiting and hard to get game with me. If you stop a minute to think about it, it is really quite cruel.

I hope you find warmth, in the years ahead, from my many words over these past months. Consider them as a wonderful gift that came from my heart and I will never regret having written them.

I was so busy blaming myself yesterday and last night for everything that it dawned on me as I was crying my eyes out sitting in the car outside the house. It is not all my fault and I am not this despicable person you may think I am. You have made me feel like I was not good enough for you and I did not deserve to be treated that way.

Now all I want is for you to be GONE BUT NOT FORGOT-TEN.

The End
Irene

This entire "end" lasted only one hour and twenty-two minutes before I thought of something else to say. I sat in front of my computer wondering if any of this had to do with the repackaging of Irene and the boldness in my newly found freedom of speech in the past months.

Sent: January 20, 2007 11:32 A.M.
Subject: P.S. The grand finale

I forgot something as usual. I was going to ask you why you chose to sing the Marley tune again on Thursday night. I think it is a fitting tune for the grand finale. Unlike what you think and say, it is not you doing the waiting, but me and you certainly haven't been knocking on my door for three years. I've been waiting for you to knock on my door in the daytime for three months.

...I know, now that I'm way down on your line (you have never made time for me)

...But the waitin' feeling is fine   (no it isn't)

...So don't treat me like a puppet on a string   (we only see each other when you say)

...I wanna know when you're gonna come   (when are you coming to Canmore?)

...Tears in my eyes burn   (they certainly are now)

...While I'm waiting for my turn   (to see you in the day)

You can't possibly think that those words are for you to say and not what I feel. You keep telling me you understand women. Explain to me. Why do many women know the words to songs and also spend a great deal of time making up their own words at operas, ballets and symphonies? Meanwhile, men only seem to be there for the music and the beat?

I love you

Irene

Chapter 45

Panic started to overcome me by mid afternoon and then he finally called. We spoke on the phone for at least an hour and I could hear the pain in his voice. He kept over and over again telling me about how much I hurt him with my betrayal.

Sent: January 20, 2007 5:50 P.M.
Subject: Hurting too!

You still think it is only you who is hurting. I am hurting since early December. I have been almost begging you in the past two months to "throw me another crumb". That crumb was a sign of affection I rarely saw, other than in bed. Women need more than that and you have claimed to know women so well and ultimately; it turns out you don't, at least not me. I told you before I am not used to someone being so secretive and unable to show there affection. That brick wall you have built around yourself is massive; it is destroying everything that could possibly be good in your life.

I questioned if it was only me in love and I was just another pastime for you. You told me many times all these women in the clubs, including here at Benny's, were coming onto you and you could have your pick. Yesterday, you told me that the other guys are always taking the women home you have your eye on. I know you told me this before, but I never really thought or felt you cared enough about me to even worry if I wound up with someone else.

That is why what happened on New Year's, happened. I really thought and felt it was over between us and I didn't expect to really see you again, which led me to the other guy. I was trying to protect myself from you because I thought you really didn't care. You had enough time to show me you did and yet you didn't. When you care about someone, you spend time with them; something you never have enough of for me. I know you were very busy in December, but don't tell me you never took an afternoon or evening off in the whole month.

What could possibly make you think Friday and Saturday night and twice on a Thursday, in three months, could be enough to make me think you really cared? I forgot about Boxing Day when you did come out here at 6:00 p.m. when I had the stomach flu.

I am going to bed now with some vodka and I am hoping it will kill the pain. I have a huge day tomorrow and I need to have dry, unpuffy eyes by then.

Love
Irene

Sent: January 20, 2007 6:10 P.M.
Subject: Worth Fighting For

I forgot to tell you I am going to bed with Bob Marley tonight, besides the vodka. I am sure I will look at the words to that tune many times tonight, while you listen to your own music.

I told you this week I was happy you turned out to be a lover and not a fighter, but you need to decide whether or not I am worth fighting for because I do love you and I need to see your love.

..........again I will be waiting!

Love and will miss you to the end of my days! (If you prove to be unworthy of my affection)

Irene

Sent: January 20, 2007 9:13 P.M.
Subject: Half a Heart?

Do you remember that I told you that I am an "all or nothing" type of girl? I told you right from the beginning you could tell me "NO", but "WHOA", I wouldn't understand. Maybe this is something you don't get completely. Whether it was the furniture store, real estate and in my everyday dealings with people, I only know one way- which is all of me or nothing. You either accept everything or you will receive nothing.

I really thought you were the person, strong enough and capable of having and accepting all of me. Maybe I was mistaken. I thought you were so wrapped up in your music that you also heard every tune and would understand where I was coming from. Maybe you haven't heard enough of the words to the songs you play; you're too caught up in the melody to actually hear any of the words.

The reason I say this is because, in order to be great at anything in life, you need to give all of yourself. I tried to teach this to my children. I don't want my children to give only half of themselves to what they undertake in life.

People, who wind up giving only half, also only receive half. If they give all, they will receive all.

With giving all, they can achieve such success in life and not only in their careers, but also in their love life. They will have piece of mind, knowing that they gave everything they had, even when they find out their loved one had fallen into bed with someone else. Don't get me wrong, because I do not condone this and I am devastated by this, as you are.

You have given me not even half of what you are capable of and you think this is all I deserve or want? Not a chance! I need more, because I tried hard to live my life more than just halfway to no-where, but mediocre. How could you possibly think that I would be satisfied with just a Friday and Saturday night between 12:30 A.M. and noon the next day?

I thought you wanted nothing and at best you only gave me half of yourself and this is another explanation for what happened to us. It appears in life, the only thing you give all of yourself to is your music. This is where you will possibly achieve success, but not in your love life with me.

Now I had too much Vodka, but it doesn't really matter because my tune never changes in life, regardless of what I drink. I've been saying the same thing for so long now, I have it memorized.

Good Night Cephus! I love you will all of my heart and not just with half of it!

Irene

Chapter 46

I finally got everything out of my system for the day and I knew the vodka helped. I could barely see the keyboard anymore, much less remember where to place my fingers and this was a good thing. I could finally go to bed now and actually sleep and I was glad the day was done. The pain, however, continued and, true to my nature, I would ultimately wind up blaming myself for everything that went wrong in the relationship from day one.

I couldn't imagine ending a relationship over the phone or in an email and I desperately wanted to hear from him. I wanted to see him one last time and very much regretted the thought that I may never hear his laugh again or his stories.

He called again that evening during one of his breaks at Benny's. It was around 10:00 and I just finished my last email to him for the day and my last vodka for the night. My heart jumped and I knew by looking at the bottle, I had had enough and I quickly jumped into the shower and shaved my legs. He was coming over when he was done playing.

By the time he arrived, the first thing he needed was a drink and I joined him. I don't remember very much of what was said, but I do remember him telling me that I needed to look in that mirror again. He generally stayed away from newly divorced women because of all the excess baggage. If our relationship was to continue, he felt he was destined to pay for all of the mistakes John had made in our marriage.

We still made love at the beginning of our evening, which totally baffled me because all he was doing was lecturing me and I was listening. I couldn't figure out why a man with so much wisdom would ever want to touch a harlot like me.

At some point during the course of the night, I do remember thinking about the woman I thought of as a simpleton. She saved my life years ago and was the reason I was still here. Maybe she or someone similar would prove to be my second salvation, but we were alone and I would have no such luck. I would have to keep it together on my own.

If I had summed up the whole evening with few words, and this would be difficult for me, I would have stated that I had felt totally responsible for everything that was not working in our relationship. I was a drunk, a whore and an evil person and I was prepared to take any shit he would dish out because I deserved it. The night of talking lasted until about 6:00 A.M. I was happy when the birds finally got up. I was exhausted, not only from listening, but also from the liquor and no sleep. I wanted his speech to end.

By morning, I forgot about anything that was ever good about myself and I wondered what the hell had happened to Mother T.? Cephus left around noon and I will never forget having to go into work when my eyes were almost swollen shut from all the tears I had shed and all the liquor I had consumed.

Part Eight
The Resurrection

Chapter 47

Sent: January 21, 2007 12:53 P.M.
Subject: Choosing a different path now

Hi

I'm waiting for clients to show up and I wanted to tell you I know I've really screwed us both up. I cannot get over the fact that my stupidity may wind up costing me possibly the best thing that's ever happened to me, which is you. I will have to figure out a way to fix it, if I can. The first step for me will be to give up drinking and the tobacco and then I will take it from there.

Irene

Sent: January 22, 2007 7:56 A.M.
Subject: Good Morning

I woke up this morning and as usual the first thing I did was think about you and I went to the computer with my coffee. Now I feel like I can't write to you because you don't want to hear from me anymore. I think to myself, I should be quiet for awhile and I find I can't. Maybe I am used to writing daily now. What do you think? Should I stop?

All I want to say is good morning and I hope your day goes well.

Love
Irene

Sent: January 22, 2007 3:02 P.M.
Subject: !@#$%^&*??.....confusion

In the quick sands my emotions have become since the betrayal, I try to say good morning to you, but I even have doubt about that because I'm thinking deep in my soul, "maybe she's having a better morning than I can imagine, with somebody NEW, AGAIN", and although everything says to me it's not fair to think of you that way, that is where I am at, at the moment and into deep mistrust.

Yesterday morning, on the drive back to town, the morning sun was in my eyes so I pulled the shade down, to protect my eyes and a sheet of paper fell down. It was the email you had written to me on the second week of January saying you were sorry and so on I had printed it out and re-read it a few times. It was a nice letter then and I had kept it because I missed you, and I just couldn't understand why day versus night had become such an ultimatum. So you were about to begin my year with such a hassle, but I was willing to make adjustments and let my guard down because I realized I cared for you and the few times when you showed me your soft side, I was falling in deeply.

When it fell from the shade yesterday, I glanced at it and then read it, and then I realized it was written a few days after you had made the decision to cheat on our relationship, and that letter, was supposed to be a lifeline to my heart, turned out to be insincere and bullshit. I just couldn't help my self I pulled to the side of the highway, stopped, sat in my car and had a good cry.

I made it to Knox United barely on time and in pretty bad shape too, but I was able to do what I was supposed to do. I'll recover from that, although I wish I didn't have any of these bitter pills to deal with.

I go to my computer and I don't know if I ever want to hear from you again and yet I look to see if you're there. Why? I don't see anything from you and instead of feeling relief I feel disappointment and then panic. Maybe she didn't care at all. Maybe she could be off with some other guy. Who knows? So I guess only you can help and in my current state, I would rather have the lies from you than the disappointment of not hearing from you. At least I will know you're on your computer......

Love and Pain

CJ

Sent: January 22, 2007 3:47 P.M.
Subject: Sharing same state...confusion/pain & on computer

God, I opened your email at work and started to cry on duty desk! I had to get someone to cover for me and so I could go outside for half an hour and give myself time to recover. Now I have so much work to do here and all I can think of is, to reply to your email.

I don't know if you still have the email I sent to you on the 5th of January, but at the bottom of it, I wrote I did not want you to phone that weekend and I would suffer through the pain of missing you, alone. It went on to say, "Come to think of it there are many people who love me day and night, you were just not one of them". "You're not one of them", tells you I really doubted your love. This is where my head was leading into the weekend.

I really believed you didn't love me. Not enough to see me during the day. I couldn't understand how I could tell you so many times and in so many different ways. This was important to me and you always ignored it, which led me to believe that I and my feelings didn't matter to you. My God, Cephus, my telling you this was important to me; it started at least in December, if not sooner. I asked you to throw me a crumb of affection in December and then on Boxing Day, you did show up earlier. The only problem there was, I actually anticipated you early in the afternoon, the daytime, and then when you called you said you would be there about 5:00. You finally showed up at 6:00 and I had that terrible stomach flu to top everything off.

Especially difficult for me, was the Christmas season, when every time that I suggested something occur in the day or early evening, you totally ignored all of it. This included the staff Christmas party, that took me two weeks to get a "NO" answer and the Christmas dinner invitation which you never answered. Then on New Year's Eve, while at Cynthia's, your call came in at about 1:20 A.M., only to tell me you would be in Canmore within twenty minutes. I rushed home with Stewart and Diane only to wind up waiting another one and one half hours for you to show up. That really hurt me. Christmas alone and here it was New Year's Eve and I felt like you didn't want to spend it with me, other than in bed and very, very late. This is what led to the hooker email. All of my confusion, about your affections for me, came crashing down from that time, but it has been a steady build up since early December.

At the New Year's Eve party, Cynthia and others were begging me not to go and they couldn't figure out why you wouldn't come there to pick me up. By 1:00 A.M., I assumed you didn't want to be there. It was getting late and I was tired. By that time, I would have rather been alone with you than with them. That is why I left. Why wouldn't you tell me that you thought I didn't want you there? I still wound up waiting much longer before you eventually showed up at home. So many drinks later, is why I wound up the next morning with such a hangover; it put me into this tailspin. I still can't believe you thought another man was waiting for me at Joanna's the next morning. Do I need to guess everything you're thinking?

The January 9th email, after the weekend without you, I wrote about my great plan to not have you call me anymore. It backfired on me and I had the weekend from hell. My plan was to drive you out of my heart because I really didn't figure that I was in yours. I thought and felt that I was the one headed for a major heartbreak. In the same email, I said I was the only one heartbroken by our weekend apart because I realized I couldn't drive you out of it. I was the one who went beyond the limits and cheated on you. In the next two weeks our relationship actually got better, which only made me feel even worse about myself and that weekend.

When we were at Buffalo's on those two nights, and you played the Marley tune, I knew in my heart that you played those songs for me. What you don't know is that each time I heard the song, I felt your love and the depths of my betrayal at the same time. It had taken so much of your love for me, to sing those songs. The next thing I knew was that I could no longer live with these lies in my head without telling you, which led us to where we are now.

Everyday, since Thursday, has been a living hell for not only you, but for me as well. Don't forget I was the cause of it and the only one to blame. The only wrongdoing on your part was the fact that you kept your heart guarded and concealed from me. I became confused about your love and it is only since the weekend that I truly see what your feelings are for me. Since Thursday and your email this morning, that brick wall of yours has come crashing down and there is your heart. I can see it now and I want it to stop breaking because with every tear you shed, my heart breaks further.

I have never broken someone's heart, to my knowledge, and never did I intend to break yours. As for trusting me again, I told you before, I could never cheat on someone and this is the truth. If I know, and I do now, that someone loves me, I don't EVER look at other men that way. There isn't one single thing I have ever said to you in all of these emails or in person that didn't come straight from my heart. The only lie ever, was the one where I told you I slept with that guy months earlier and I couldn't even last a day with that lie much longer.

The rest of what happens to us now is up to you. All I ever wanted from the beginning and, especially now, is to have you in my arms and you need to figure out if that is where you want me to be. I will wait for you to decide what you want.

Love and Pain
Irene

P.S. If you are looking for me in the evenings after dinner, you will find me hiding in my bedroom.

The movie,"Titanic", was one of Julianna's and my favourites and I will never forget the words as Jack was sinking, while Rose was calling back, "Jack, Jack, come back". My heart screamed these words in silence to Cephus. Would it be the strength of this man's character and all of his wisdom, or the power of my words that would bring us back together from the depths of hell? All I knew was there was a new day ahead of us and above all else we needed to forget yesterday.

Sent: January 23, 2007 10:32 A.M.
Subject: Ouch!!!!

Good day Irene,

It was good to hear from you, although I still can't understand why. I don't even understand why I would want to understand, which adds to the confusion within me and even the continuing implication that somehow I am responsible for my own betrayal, which keeps adding more layers to my wall, as you call it. It is still good to hear from you.

I'm trying to have a busy week and my mind keeps drifting to us. You write your thoughts on paper and it sounds great and idealistic and loving, but you also act erratically and this throws me for a loop. Me and my thoughts come from dialogue and immediacy and I know when people don't want to listen to me and I've said that to you in the middle of our conversations and I shut down too. I've told you that many times.

I don't know what I want for us either, but right now, with all these heavy and painful and mistrusting feelings, I carry for the relationship, I know I still don't want to let it go.

Like I said before, I'm having a busy, but unproductive week, as I know that you did my head in. I'm doing the Delta Bow, which means it's gonna be rush, rush from the Delta to Buffalo's on Thursday night. I'm planning to drive to DMF after the Delta on Wednesday, tomorrow, to pick up my gear. More importantly, to see you and see if we can continue to salvage what's left of us. If that's ok with you, I should be in Canmore about 8:30–9:00 P.M., if you have not chosen to replace me by then.

Still more pain than love
Cephus

The next four days it became apparent that neither one of us wanted the relationship to end. We began to try and patch things back together. He called and said that the more I wrote and explained to him the reasons for my actions, the easier it may be for him to forget, forgive and for us to move on, but the blow had been swift and hard. He assured me he would recover, mainly because he couldn't let a woman get to him as I had. Not at his age.

Early in the relationship, he had said that he was approaching the golden years alone and I got the impression that this was not how he wanted it. He married the woman of his dreams, all those years back. When it didn't work and the host of others who followed didn't work, he was almost thinking he should give up trying to find someone special, until I came along. I was only happy with the opportunity of discovering who this man really was and I was given another chance to see if we could really be together.

Christmas and the blues came and left and a New Year had begun. With this came a renewed hope that I may soon find the answers to my many questions. If my betrayal hadn't killed the relationship, then possibly nothing would and maybe we were meant to be together.

Sent: January 26, 2007 8:54 A.M.
Subject: Oh Happy Day!

Oh Happy Day!...or should I say, oh another happy day. I still can't believe I get to have you out here twice in one week before midnight and this does make me happy. Now I am a believer of your love for me. I can see the effort you are making and it will be worth it for what we are creating. Together we will chase these clouds away and I know we will mostly both have good days from now.

I still haven't figured out what to do tonight, but during the course of the day I will figure something out. I am not really used to us going out; this is why I have the dilemma. Maybe we will just have dinner here and then go to Bearin's for a bit, or I could see if Lily and Peter are doing anything and we could meet up with them in Banff. I hope you have a good day with Jordon today and you actually will be able to spend some time with him. More importantly, I hope slowly and bit by bit, you are resolving all these horrible thoughts of me in your head and soon you will be able to make peace with them. Then we can move on from here to a better place.

I did wind up writing an offer yesterday, but unfortunately we got beat out by another. Now we will have to find something else for my buyers. When I do, I get to list their condo here and there is a likelihood of a referral for their place in Calgary. Today I have to get the woman in England to finally write so I have to get to the office. I was tempted to phone her again in the middle of the night, but I had such a good sleep, I couldn't get up until 7:00. I also find out today if my West Africans can remove the financing condition on their offer for the Banff property. At least the other condo deal is done, as they were preapproved for financing. That was just listed last Friday and it sold by Tuesday. I didn't even get a chance to put up a sign.

I know you missed the Coldwell Banker office. It is so easy to spot. All you have to do is look for the ugliest building on Main Street. I told my broker last summer he should consider moving or have the owner of the building renovate it. It is really quite disgusting and I think it does affect the business of the office.

Now I have to get to work, earlier than yesterday. See you later.

Love
Irene

Sent: January 26, 2007 9:16 A.M.
Subject: Trying....

I just got your note, thanks. Right now, in my mental and emotional state, I don't want our evening to include a drive from Banff to Canmore. That's still too raw for me, so if you love me, don't plan to include Banff. I'm trying to shut out thoughts in my head, so I don't always have to continually say things that sound mean and bitter. I hope you will understand.

See you later

Love
Cephus

Sent: January 26, 2007 9:54 A.M.
Subject: Banff? Where's that?

Forget Banff! We will stay in Canmore for sure, as I do love you!

Irene

Chapter 48

Sent: January 27, 2007 6:16 P.M.
Subject: The Why

Do you know, I am fifty-three years old and no one has ever asked me to open up my heart and let them in, except you? It makes me wonder, why has no one ever asked me before? The answer is there has never been anyone who really cared, until you. I can't begin to tell you how all the things you have told me this past week, tear my heart out for what I did to you. I almost wish I were dead. I could just crawl into a hole and die.

One thing I do know is I have wound up being hurt by nearly every relationship I have ever been in. Why? I don't know. Maybe it is something I bring on myself, like you said about your failed ones. I have always been the one who was left. I know it is what I thought would happen this time with you. Why should you turn out to be any different than the rest? Everyone tends to love me and leave me. Maybe I have programmed myself for failure in relationships. All I know is I love you so much and I just want to be with you all of the time. This past week, with both of us sick about each other, the only place I want to be is in your arms. It is the ONLY place I feel good. Remember what I told you this morning that you and I have never really had sex. We have only made love. The problem I have is that I had no idea how deep your love for me was until now. Had I not been so blind, none of this would have happened.

I love you and please don't give up on me.

Irene

The nights we were spending together were difficult and yet full of love. He told me how big his heart was and there was never a man in my life who could love me more than he did. Many of the stories he told these months, no one knew, not even Greg; but he shared them with me. How could I not see all this love? It had taken him years to open up to a woman again and unfaithfulness was my reaction.

The night of Cynthia's party, I hadn't asked him to pick me up and he assumed I didn't want him to, maybe because he was black. As a result, he purposely stayed later at Benny's. He insinuated somehow I didn't find him worthy of my love and he asked why I wouldn't let him discover the real me inside. He also thought this was the reason why, it appeared to him, I rushed through our lovemaking.

Cephus kept trying to extract from me what had possessed me that night to take the cab ride home. I kept thinking that I had the answer, but then Cephus would dig deeper and the conversation would go on for hours. We were both trying so hard, which in hindsight may have made things even more difficult. He kept insisting that I look in my mirror for the answers and that I dig deeper into my heart and soul to see why I had hurt such a kind and loving man.

Part Nine
Self Analysis

Chapter 49

Sent: January 28, 2007 9:24 A.M.
Subject: Be Happy

Some days you have to write those words over and over again as a person may need to be reminded, like me this morning. I slept from 8:00 last night until 8:00 this morning and I am still exhausted. I will have to go to bed early again tonight and maybe then I will get caught up with my sleep.

I think in order for me to clear up, in my own head and possibly yours, "the why" of the cab ride home that night, I have to revisit some of my past relationships. When I wrote to you yesterday, the words, "I have always been the one who was left", I thought this could be a clue for us.

Relationship #1: I was seventeen and dating this black belt from Calgary for about eight months and he was begging me to have sex with him. I kept refusing, saying as soon as I would give myself to him, he would leave me. He kept pestering me about it so I decided to consult my girlfriends whether I should or shouldn't.

There were about five or six of us having coffee in Banff and I still haven't forgotten that day. I can still hear and see them looking at me in amazement and laughing. They had all, except one, been having sex for years. I remember being shocked to discover this and I figured that they couldn't all be stupid and, in fact, I thought they were all generally smarter than I. I gave in to my boyfriend and we had sex twice.

A couple of months later, we were sitting in his car and he was telling me he loved me, but he needed a break from the relationship. I fought back the tears, but one did manage to escape. I remember thinking about how well I had taken it on the surface. I really should have listened to my mother in the first place and not have given in to his sexual urges.

What really made it easier for me was that two girlfriends and I were flying to Mexico the next month and the excitement of the trip should have helped me to get over him. A couple of months later, he was knocking on my door and wanting to get back into my life and heart, because he thought he had made a mistake. I told him I wasn't interested. He broke my heart once and I was not about to let it happen again.

By this time, I had graduated from high school and moved to Calgary with a girlfriend and my younger sister, Rose. We were frequenting the bars by then and experimenting with pot and other drugs. That night when she told me that I didn't know "where it was at", was what actually led me to experiment with the drugs in the first place.

Years later, I found myself in Kenya on a safari and we spotted this monkey sitting on a stump in the middle of nowhere. He sat there crosslegged, with his hands clasped in his lap and he looked out onto the felled trees left by the elephants that had passed. I asked the driver to stop so I could have a closer look at this animal that appeared deep in thought. I got out of the van and as I looked through the lens of the camera, the greying monkey turned his head ever so slowly and our eyes met. I will never forget the look and what I felt those eyes were telling me. He looked at me and asked what it was I was staring at. He was really the one that possessed all the wisdom. I believed him and thought of my sister's words that day in the cabin.

Looking back on that time, I believe it was an attempt, on my part, to be bad for a change and to see what it was like. Relationship #1 wanted to start things up again, which brought back the whole pain of his leaving. What did I do? I wound up sleeping with a guy I knew from the bar and I got pregnant. At this point, I had only slept with relationship #1. To top things off, I had an abortion on Mother's

180

day and I moved back to Banff and to celibacy.

I have to go to work now. The call came in about the offer I am working on and we have to accept or counter it before noon today. I will continue with this in the afternoon.

Sent: January 28, 2007 5:15 P.M.
Subject: to continue….

You see, after this first relationship floundered, I actually started to think seriously again about becoming a nun and never having sex with another man. Even while in Mexico, there were several opportunities, but I had been quick to make up the rule that none of us would date without the other two present at all times. Consequently, we were never alone with any of the men. I even turned down an invitation from a famous Mexican sculptor. He offered to fly me in his private jet from Mexico City to Acapulco and, instead, I wound up with my girlfriends on the six hour bus ride with the chickens. In Acapulco, the three of us hung around with about six guys from various countries and none of us so much as let them steal a kiss.

I tried hard to live a spiritual life, close to God. Saying my prayers at night with my sister was an important part of my childhood. Mother Teresa was my mentor and I thought He would forgive me and my single indiscretion at the time. If I followed in the footsteps of MT, it would allow me to continue to travel and maybe to make a difference in the world, as she had. Once the abortion and the drugs came, I assumed I was soiled for life and my path would be forever altered, even though I remained spiritual. I never again felt that I was good enough for the calling. This hurt me deeply, as I cared so much for the people around me and I tried hard to always be good.

From the young age of fourteen, I found myself giving counsel to others on their sexual issues with their parents and their friends. I was still a virgin and with absolutely no experience and yet they seemed to listen to me as if I somehow had all the answers.

In the first place, the whole reason that Rose was living with us was because my parents were at a loss as to what to do with her. She was sent for me to watch over and, in the end, it was me who needed the guidance. She wound up married at seventeen and I had failed. My brother also had his share of problems which I tried to sort out, including his drug problems and his wife who had left him.

People seemed to be always asking me for advice. My boss and his wife in Banff were asking me what to do with their teenage son and my advice seemed to work for them for awhile, but they refused to get professional help for him. Years later, I found out that he had ultimately committed suicide and I was sad, but not surprised.

Relationship #2 came along after the abortion and I was no where near ready for that one. I was going to Europe again with another girlfriend and we were not certain when we would return. This was one of the few relationships in my life that I actually ended, other than a brief one with a banker that was nonsexual, before the "big first".

#2 was leading to marriage which threw me for a loop. This was the last thing on my mind at the time as we hadn't even been seeing each other for long. This was 1972 and he did actually contact me years later, in the mid 80s. He had moved back to Switzerland shortly after our relationship had ended. He flew to Toronto from Switzerland on business and one of those men flew all the way from Toronto just to buy me dinner. Out of curiosity, I did have dinner with him and, during the course of the meal, I realized that I hadn't made a mistake. Food was all we shared that night.

Immediately after the end of this second relationship and prior to my next trip to Europe, I wound up in the Catholic Church in Banff and on my knees. I asked God to forgive my sins of the previous year and to please send me a man to love and who would love me in return. The very next day, I met a man where I worked and I believed he was sent from heaven. He turned out to be a real swindler and #3. He was extremely good looking and told me he was an American from Florida and was drafted to play in the NHL for the Edmonton Oilers. I believed him. He had a criminal record the length of his arm, for swindling women out of their money. He turned out to be the silver tongued devil. I lost $800.00 and another little piece of my pride and my heart.

My girlfriend and I, after travelling through Germany and France, wound up in Malaga, Spain, where we rented an apartment. We both quickly found boyfriends and mine was a med student from Venezuela who was taking a year off from university. He was the DJ in the popular disco there and #4. I quickly fell in love with him only to find out later that he was actually in love with some fifteen year old whose parents would not let them date. Apparently, he was waiting until she turned sixteen so they could be married. By the time I was ready to come back home, he started falling in love with me and he was tired of waiting for the other girl. I didn't find out until years later that my father had burned all the many letters that this guy had sent to me after my return. My father thought I would hop onto the next plane and be lost forever.

I must have still had Spain in my heart, because relationship # 5 was a Spanish soccer player who had recently immigrated to Calgary. We were not together very long and, in the end, it turned out that I wasn't what he was looking for and so we broke up and I moved back to Banff. I remember feeling that I was just not good enough for him; but, boy, could we dance together.

Relationship #6 lasted over two years and was with a member of the R.C.M.P. who worked in undercover narcotics in Banff. We seemed to get along well and I don't recall ever having a real fight with him. We did a great deal of hiking, skiing, biking and just playing cards together. It was the most peaceful relationship until he got transferred back into Calgary and it became a long distance romance. Eventually, I also left Banff and moved back into Calgary to be closer to him. The spark had faded. So I flew to Europe and Africa for a couple of months, to give him time to think.

He eventually told me he wasn't happy with the relationship so we decided to end it. The funny thing about the end is, that although it was his idea, he kept phoning and coming around as if nothing had happened. I asked him three times to stop calling until he eventually did stop. I was not the one who was unhappy and, in fact, he had envisioned the wedding with me in white and with him in his red serge. Again I was left heartbroken. The only way to a man's heart is through his stomach and all those years of my learning how to cook Ukrainian food, hadn't help this relationship.

No one has been in the office all afternoon and it is now almost 5:00 and time to lock up.

My sweet father brought me some lunch an hour ago so I actually have eaten something today before 8:00 P.M., the first time all week. They are all worried I am losing far too much weight.

This could be continued later from home, if I don't go to bed straight away. Maybe I will have a quick nap. I am on floor duty again in the morning and have the office phones tonight. Sorry this is so long; but you did want to know who I am inside. Unfortunately, I believe my past relationships have helped shape the future ones and I think that this is the only way that we are going to get to the bottom of this. Remember, you can tell me anytime you want to stop and I will.

I love you and miss you today. Actually, I had a couple of little stirrings down there today, so I guess I am not totally dead inside yet.

Irene

Sent: January 28, 2007 10:06 P.M.
Subject: Good night

I know I said I would write again tonight, but I can't. I came home, had a cry and a bowl of soup and a short nap and then I watched one and one half love stories on the women's network and I cried again during both of them. Neither one of them turned out well. Now I need to sleep.

I'll probably get up early and write again. I forgot to tell you that the deal I was working on yesterday, got accepted. That makes two this week.

Good night

Love
Irene

Chapter 50

Sent: January 29, 2007 7:50 A.M.
Subject: Be Happy it's Monday

I wonder why I like Mondays, so much? Maybe it is because Mondays are at the beginning and beginnings are generally a good thing. On the other hand, it could be when you rarely take a day off, Monday is the beginning of something fresh and last week's business is hopefully taken care of.

Joanna called me last night to see how I was doing. She phoned on Saturday night, as well, and asked about how our date went the night before. I didn't have the heart to tell her that it had started out well with dinner at Three Sister's and then it had turned sour. I didn't tell her you woke up and bolted out of bed at 4:00 in the morning in tears and that we both cried until 5:00. I only told her it went all right and we were still working things out. It is a good thing she didn't see me on Saturday or she would have known something was wrong.

She asked me last night if I had heard from you and I said no. I told her you wanted me to continue writing so you could really get to know me. I said I sent you about five or six pages yesterday and she wondered what the hell I could talk about for so long. She figures that by now you already have a book on me.. Little does she know that there are many things that we still need to discuss.

Similar to life, I think that in relationships, the harder the work put in, the greater the rewards in the end. This morning's first cup of coffee brought that to mind, when I thought of all the work that I did last week. Steve, my broker, told me yesterday that the reason I was doing so well was because I was doing everything right and that made me feel good. He wondered what was wrong with me on Saturday and I told him that I worked too hard last week, I needed a day off and I was having problems in my love life. What he didn't know was, that although I may be doing everything right at work, I certainly hadn't been doing things right with you and this relationship.

Now I am thinking that the harder we work at this and once we get things figured out, we may really have something that most people would only dream of. Similar to real estate, I am prepared to do whatever it takes to make it work. All I know is, from what I have seen in you these last two weeks, I should be prepared to write another one hundred pages. If this is what it will take, then I will do it. It is certainly a switch from me and my wanting to end it a few short weeks ago. It will be more difficult for you to get rid of me now.

You see, Cephus, when your wall came crashing down and your soul was exposed to me, I couldn't believe my eyes. I have caught a glimpse now of all of your strengths and your weaknesses and I see the power of the love you are capable of and I am left in awe. I want you now more than ever because I believe I have finally found someone whose depth of being and passion, matches my own.

Could I be so foolish or stupid to take another cab ride, after watching you bolt out of bed crying about what I had done? My only wish is that I would have seen it before and I could have saved us both from the grief we have suffered since then.

Not a good way to end this morning, but I do have to get into the shower and get to work. Did Jordon leave yesterday? It would be nice if you gave me a call sometime. I will try to continue from yesterday, later at work.

I love you
Irene

Sent: January 29, 2007 10:17 A.M.
Subject: Hi...the why...the who

Hi Irene,

I spent a hectic day, mostly with Jordon and his musical stuff, but I finally got him on the red-eye at 12:50 A.M. He is going to be alright I think, now that he sees that I'm ok.

Am I ok? I still don't know. I knew there was mail from you and I eagerly got to them, when I got back from the airport. I'm glad, in a way, you are putting this on paper, the why and I really don't want you to stop, because maybe in finding out the why, which are circumstances, I might be able to discover the who, the person who attracts me, gives me a pitch about virtues, invites me into her life, says she loves me, taints it with haste and ultimatum, watches as I fall for her, never gives me a real chance and then cruelly breaks my heart by cheating, before we could get it together.

Yes, if the why can help me find, the who, who still has my love, it could also eventually help to rebuild trust and forgiveness in my soul.

I notice you just sent mail. I haven't opened it yet, but I'm sending this anyway.

Luv
Cephus

Part Ten
One Step at a Time

Chapter 51

Sent: January 29, 2007 12:50 P.M.
Subject: Thank you

Thank you for calling me this morning. I couldn't say, "I love you" back, as both the secretary and Steve were both within earshot. I love you back!

I have this poem hanging at my desk in the office and I thought I would send it to you. I've had it for a number of years and have given it to many people and I thought you might like it as well. It is good for just about everything in life, including relationships. I hope you are able to print it.

I will be very happy to see you on Wednesday. I will write again this afternoon as I keep getting interrupted. My back is totally shot today and I can barely sit, so I will have to figure out how to fix that first.

Love
Irene

Sent: January 29, 2007 3:04 P.M.
Subject: ???????!!!!!

I got your poem and I'm even more confused now. I have to put this question to you and I'd rather you wait until I see you on Wednesday to get your reply. So think about it, but you can continue on your "Why" to me.

The question is how could you possess such a poem, believe it, email it to your friends and to me, and yet fail to do any of the things that the poem suggests with regards to our relationship? And you profess to love me? Do you remember, whoa and slow down, so I can see you, taste you, appreciate you. What was the rush? Even the sex was rushed and when I didn't respond as quickly as you would have liked, look at what the haste led you to do.

AND YOU HAD THIS POEM ALL ALONG

????????

Cephus

The poem I sent was called "One Step at a Time" by Lucille Boesken. By the sounds of his email, I should have kept it to myself. Why is it when a person falls in love, they sometimes forget things they have possibly known inside of themselves for years? Obviously, Cephus was right again and I felt foolish. I was rushing everything with us. Now it would take another ten pages to diagnose the "why" for sending the poem. I still wasn't tired of writing to him and I continued with my self analysis. Considering the number of pages that spewed out of me over this short period of time, I guess I was trying to rush this as well. I wanted to get the pain dealt with and over with.

Sent: January 29, 2007 3:16 P.M.
Subject: Older and Wiser

I rarely sit at that desk at work, as it used to be Mary's. I walked passed it this morning and spotted the poem again. I haven't looked at it since before her funeral. It wasn't until this morning and I was sending it to you, that it dawned on me, that it also could relate to relationships. Every time I ever read it before, I only thought of the other aspects of life to which it pertained, but never to relationships.

Some things you will just have to teach ME. After all, you are older than I am and are supposed to be wiser. Now I am crying again. The poem has new meaning for me today. Thank you for the lesson.

Love
Irene

Sent: January 30, 2007 1:38 A.M.
Subject: More than bedtime now

I have spent a whole hour now writing to you and I have saved it into my drafts because I can't finish it tonight. I may have time before the 9:00 A.M. staff meeting. Anyway, the email started from where I left off the last one, with tears after the poem, shopping with Jessica, more work, another cry and then a nap, then cooking for six kids, a heart to heart talk with my mother, a drink with Joanna, an hour trying to explain the day and evening to you and now I am exhausted and I need to go to bed.

It was the heart to heart with my mother that really got to me and I will have to explain it to you tomorrow. Anyway, I told her everything that has been going on with us in the last month. As usual and to be expected, she was very understanding and totally sympathetic to your cause. I will tell you the whole thing tomorrow or on Wednesday. Suffice it to say, at the end of our discussion, her advice to me was to go straight home and send you an email, which, of course, I couldn't because Joanna called while I was there, begging me to come over. I went over for an hour and then came home.

The rest of this will have to come later, as I am, once again, emotionally exhausted. All I can think of is how upset you are with me again, because I didn't have the same interpretation of the poem as you did. All those years, like you said, I read it and gave it away and I had never associated it with a relationship until this morning and until you.

Love
Irene

191

Chapter 52

Sent: January 30, 2007 8:47 A.M.
Subject: Running Late

I slept in this morning and I am running behind. I will have a relatively light day today and hopefully tomorrow. This will be sort of like having days off. I only have to update all the photos for the windows and walls in the office, attend a staff meeting and an open house tour.

I should have time this afternoon to finish the email I started late last night and I will continue with where I left off on the Sunday one. I hope you woke up this morning with love in your heart for me and not too upset.

In your email yesterday, you were so annoyed because you said I also rushed our lovemaking, which I know has upset you before on numerous occasions. This is something I definitely need help with, as I know it is true. Only one person in my life slowed me down for that and it wasn't my last relationship. I would really like it if you brought me back to that space. The question is do you have the patience to teach me?

Till later.....have a good day

Love
Irene

Sent: January 30, 2007 10:41 A.M.
Subject: Pssst

Good Morning,

You keep asking me about my love for you throughout this ordeal. This person who you JILTED, and who still looks forward to your emails, hoping to find out who you really are and who is still trying to understand the chasm between "your words" and "your actions", which so far, well, we don't want to keep belabouring that point, do we?

The only thing that keeps me wanting to try to go on is love for the ideal of you. It's the only thing I've got going, not trust, not sincerity, just love, but as Bob Marley asks in another song, "Could you be loved?"......

Cephus

Sent: January 30, 2007 6:41P.M.
Subject: Pssst yourself

I am still in the office and have not finished my work from this morning, so much for a half day off. I am meeting clients here later to write an offer, but not until 8:00 tonight. When I read your "pssst", an interesting thought came into my head. Have you ever really forgiven the other two women in your life who cheated on you? I question whether you really had or not, as I am not sure. This led me to Google the word "forgiveness" to see exactly what would come up. You should have a look at it, if you get a chance, as it was interesting. It is the fifth one down when you get there. It says, "Forgiveness", what is it for, by none other than Larry James. It would have to be a Larry.

I never visited the site before, never having done much in my life to warrant seeking forgiveness and naturally he chose to open with a quote from one of my favourite people, Mother T, "If we really want to love, we must learn how to forgive". Jilted, cheated, untrustworthy, insincere and all words never before used to describe me and now here they are, spoken in the same breath with my name and they are making me sick to hear them.

Did you really mean the part about how you don't think I have been sincere? What I didn't have time to tell you last night, was why I had gone over to my mother's. I couldn't stand another day without being forgiven by someone. You were not forgiving me and I wasn't forgiving myself either and I can't afford to lose my health over this.

That is why I wound up telling her the whole story and she surprised me by telling me she suspected something. I cried my eyes out and she forgave me and told me she thought you would too, but it would take time, like you said. She told me to go home and write to you. What I wondered was, if you, in fact, haven't forgiven the first two, then I don't have a hope in hell of being forgiven by you either. That thought is very depressing for me.

In my discussion with her, I asked her why, in life, I never was allowed to make any mistakes. People always seemed to expect me to have all the answers, even to the questions I should not know anything about. They expected that because I appeared to know everything, I was also incapable of making any of my own mistakes.. It seems that for any mistakes that I have made in the past, I have paid dearly for them. None of these, though, ever entailed intentionally hurting people.. That just wasn't in my nature and they generally only hurt me. The biggest mistakes I have made tended to always relate to my bad judgment of someone else's character and to my trustworthy nature. This has always been my downfall. I have been okay picking tenants for rental units, but I have not done so well in choosing, in my life, the men I would love.. I tend to see only the good in people and choose to ignore the majority of their flaws. My theory is that we all have flaws. So why dwell on them?

Sorry, if this seems fragmented; but I have stopped and started this about eight times and I tend to lose my train of thought. Now the office is closed and I am by myself again, so I should be able to focus better. However, it is 6:00 and the appliance repair man phoned and he is going to my house to fix the dryer and I need to go home and feed the kids. There will be only three at home tonight and I do need to be back here by 8:00 to write the offer, so I am still rushed…….the story of my life.

Actually, this is not far from the truth about being rushed all of my life. I have always moved at a fast clip, because I generally did the work of at least two people. Partly, because it was the way I was raised and from my past work experience. Can I slow down? I have slowed down considerably in the last two years and I would love to slow down even more and the passing of time and aging most likely will help. If not, maybe I will need assistance from friends and someone who loves me, like you.

By the way, the ideal you have of me, is me. I just have to figure out how to show you. Does this have to be rushed or do I have time? The last question I have for you is, do you and, can you, forgive people when they make mistakes?

I love you and I am looking forward to being with you tomorrow. I only hope we can relax together and not spend the whole night dwelling on the ugly subject of cheating, jilting and so on.

Love
Irene

P.S. I may write more to you later if I get done at a reasonable hour.

Chapter 53

Sent: January 30, 2007 8:15 P.M.
Subject: I'm back in the office

My clients just phoned from Banff, as I was leaving the house and they cancelled on me. There will be no offer tonight. I left my briefcase open and the lights on in the office and so here I am. I think I'll stay awhile because it is so quiet right now and not so at home.

You did not sound good on the phone before and you have me worried. I detected a sense of urgency in your voice. You either wanted to see me or just to talk, but I hate telephones, did you know that? I wish it was tonight you were coming out here and not tomorrow. You seem so far away.

I spent years at the furniture store with a phone hanging on my ear. When I sold the store to stay home, I was so happy when the phone rang and I didn't have to answer it. It used to drive everyone crazy, but usually my hands were in the bread dough or up on a ladder, hammer in hand and the phone down below. I always said I would be happy to die, never having owned a cell phone and here I find I can't live without it.

You know you needn't wonder why I didn't believe all the nice things you said to me before, as you are the first to say these things to me. Most of the men in my past said nothing. Many of the men in my life made me feel like they were killing time, while they were waiting for the right one to come along, or maybe this was just in my own mind.

That was, the way it appeared with relationship #7. My birthday had come along and I was expecting an engagement ring, because it appeared we had got along well. He even invited me along on a vacation with his parents and sister. This was the two hundred pound sister I spoke of before. I wound up having to sleep with her in the upper bunk of a Winnebago. No wonder I prefer five star hotels to camping. Anyway, I received a bottle of perfume, instead of the ring, and we both agreed to go our separate ways.

Did you know that I had spent a whole year living in Calgary, in about 1975? I was the assistant manager for a tuxedo rental and men's made-to-measure suit company. The manager was a male model in Calgary and most of his friends were models as well. You should like this story, as it is also true.

Needless to say, working in a place like this, opportunities abounded. I used to joke about it all the time with my girlfriends and about how for a living I got to measure men's inseams. I also met all those "best men" in the wedding parties. The joke was: I had a theory that a person should never date someone they meet through work. I wonder if relationship #3 had anything to do with this or maybe the Mother. It was certainly a stupid theory, not even one that my girlfriends could talk me out of. I turned all of these men down, including my boss's friends. The biggest part of the joke is that I never had a single date that whole year and I wondered why. The year ended with my thoughts that there was something terribly wrong with me.

That was the year, Jennifer, a friend from high school, and I used to go out at least once or twice a week to places like Old Bailey's, Lucifer's, the Sport's Club and Ranchman's. We were all over the map and neither one of us had a date that year. She just moved back from Vancouver, where she had tried modelling and it wasn't as if we were difficult to look at. I think we probably gave off this aura of "you're not going to get anything, so don't even try". Neither one of us had sex that year. By the end of it, we both flew to Club Med in Martinique, where I tried to make up for lost time. To this day, I don't remember ever seeing our room, except at check-in and check-out. She suggested a cruise and I told her that, on a ship with a bunch of grey haired people, was the last place she would find me that year. The cruise was something we could do much later in life, when we had also become grey. She, on the other hand, managed to wind up in her own bed each night and at a decent hour.

I'm going to send this to you now in hopes that you are there reading the last one and I will go home and work on the next page. If you are there, get a coffee and I will continue, because I won't be able to type as fast as you can read. I want to get the past relationships over with. Give me a few minutes though.

Back in a flash

Love
Irene

Sent: January 30, 2007 10:15 P.M.
Subject: The more things change….

I'm back. Okay, the more things change, the more they stay the same. I give up talking to the stove, only to wind up talking to the computer. This leads me to think, maybe I am rusty talking to………

You know, I spent the last eighteen years rarely talking to John, as he never seemed to be around to listen. I think the last time we spoke to each other was when forty family members and friends flew by helicopter up Heart Mountain to listen to John and I take our vows and, even that was questionable. When he was around, he could be found in bed with his eyes closed, watching television and the sports channel, of course. Maybe this is why you think I write better than I can talk. I had spent all those married years having great conversations with my children and my parents, each and every day. When they weren't around, the stove had to listen because I have always had a great deal to say about things in life.

The only problem was I somehow never had those conversations with my men. Don't get me wrong. In those first few years of my marriage I really did try very hard, but it didn't take me long to discover that my breath was wasted, as he had told me. I became quiet for the better part of the remainder of the marriage. This is probably why, towards the end, he accused me of not caring about him. I do know he used to complain bitterly when I refused to argue or fight with him and, instead, I stayed silent for the most part. This seemed to aggravate him even more. I prefer to view the relationship as war and peace and leave it at that.

I am proud that, other than a five day furniture conference in Vegas, I had never missed one single day of conversing at length with my children.. John insisted on us staying extra days and once on a three day trip to New York. So many meaningful conversations in my life, with so many different people, in so many different countries and with so many different cultures involved. Many of them were with men, but not with ones I was intimately involved with.

The others and, most likely paramount, of these conversations in life, have been with God, each morning with that first cup of coffee and cigarette. Usually I'd just thank Him for everything I had in life. I never once recall asking Him for a favour or to grant me a wish. All I ever remember was that I gave Him thanks for my many blessings from the day before and asked Him for the insight to find the blessings of the coming day.

Do you realize, in those eighteen years, I never had had a girlfriend until the latter part of the marriage? Unfortunately one died of cancer, two years into our friendship. We used to sit on my back porch and share conversations and a couple of my cigarettes a week. She never smoked and never bought any, but she was always one to enjoy someone else's. I use to tell John to take her to some of the many functions that he booked so that I could stay home and be with my children.

When she passed away, only Roxanne was left. She rented one of my cabins next door and we also shared conversations and cigarettes. I did know many people back then and we socialized a great deal. I did have my B&B guests to talk to, but it isn't really the same as they were never here very long.

To have an intimate conversation with a man hasn't happened in so many years. Maybe I am nervous and rusty, but I am sure it will come back to me. After all, if I can write so many intimate things to you, I should be able to speak them as well. I must be willing to try or I wouldn't be practising so much with all of these emails. I know that all the things that I've written to you I have not spoken out loud to anyone and, in most cases, I have avoided thinking about them.

When I typed that "period", I thought to myself, I will try to start tomorrow when you are here. Fear came to my mind. I wonder if

I will be able to open my mouth and speak tomorrow. We'll see. I think once I open the gate, it will come pouring out and it won't stop. I wonder how long it will take me. Can I take another break? I'm not tired, but my feet are freezing down here and I need a pair of socks. Please don't tell me I am all over the map again and am jumping up and down too much.

I won't be long

Love
Irene

Sent: January 30, 2007 11:35 P.M.
Subject: Longer than expected

Jason, a co-worker, just phoned from Hawaii to get an update on how his clients are doing. I am looking after them while he is away. My cell bill will be a big one this month as he has phoned at least six or seven times since he left. Thank God he will be back on Saturday and hasn't been gone long.

Everyone has gone to bed now, so we are alone. I have my socks on so most likely...nothing will happen. I think I will try to take the whole day off tomorrow, as I am acting delusional now. I have been like this most of the day, confusing all sorts of things and not remembering others and quite often, with a tear in my eye. I mixed up #6 and #7, I think, but does it really matter? After all, I am getting older too and my memory is fading. I always said this was the reason we were supposed to have children. After a while, they are supposed to take over the remembering part for us.

I had this discussion with a friend once, who never had children. She blurted out one day that she thought that she had made a big mistake by not having any children. That was the one major thing she regretted in her life. I remember telling her that if we didn't have children, who was going to miss us when we were gone? Come to think of it, I was "happily" married at the time and I am wondering why I didn't think that my husband would miss me when I was dead.

I have no more cigarettes now in the house and my mother is not

201

home. I will have to stick a patch on in the morning and give it a try. Hopefully, I will make it until evening. That will be difficult, as I don't think this is the right time for me to try to quit. I have enough stress to deal with right now in trying to make things right between us.

Relationship #8 was the Conference Director at the Banff Centre and it lasted over a year. It ended very much the same way as the last few and, in many ways, it was similar to that of the policeman. We did do a great deal of biking, hiking and skiing together. We remained friends after it ended and he moved to Vancouver. I went to visit him while he was attending law school there. He got upset when I refused to sleep with him and I ultimately decided he wasn't a good friend after all.

Now comes the difficult part, as my relationships seemed to all go downhill from there. I started the store when I was twenty-six, single and with no time for a serious relationship. You can't imagine what it is like for a single woman in a man's world of furniture. I was working on average, about sixty to seventy hours per week with absolutely no time for anything but work and no money left to top things off. Those beginning years bankrupt most people starting out in business. Well, it didn't bankrupt me, but it certainly toughened my skin and maybe this has played a role in my general hardness and many people's first impression of me at the time.

I opened the store just prior to the recession of the early 80s. Those first years, my parents wanted to know what I wanted for Christmas. I got what I asked for which was shampoo, toothpaste, soap, makeup and all the things I needed and couldn't afford any longer. Do you know from 1980 until 1989, my annual vacation was three consecutive days off each year? Maybe this is why I don't understand "slow". I do know what "fast" is.

In the beginning I was sick of people in the industry, Canmore business people and banks, treating me as if I were a joke and expecting me to go bankrupt any day. I couldn't even get a credit card for a number of years and I never borrowed a nickel in my life before. Within the first five years, the banks were begging me to borrow and I refused to even have a line of credit for the first ten years.

Over time, I managed to gain a great deal of respect in the industry and within the community. I just didn't know how to quit. This is how I met my current boss, Steve. He and I were in the Chamber together and when I had to decide on which real estate company to work for, he was the only one really keen on taking this "old" woman. He knew how hard I worked on the Chamber and the various town committees.

The year I was President of the Chamber, there were a number of people asking me to run for mayor. My business was picking up steam and I decided my energies were better spent there. I had no trouble turning them down. I spent two full years, single- handed, in trying to get an airport established for Canmore and I failed due to government cutbacks. The hundreds of hours I spent on this task left me beaten. That is when I met John and the Olympics were coming to Canmore.

Julianna spent the first twelve months of her life going to work with me each day. She was so well behaved and quiet, that you would never know that she was there. When Danny was born a year later and so premature, I hired a manager. John came into the store to help that first year and the kids stayed home with the live- in nanny. I took myself out of the public eye and proceeded to do all the "dirty" work of deliveries, repair and assembly. I will never forget when my accountant asked me when I would be ready to take the reigns again and clean house. I offered management part time employment which they declined and I left. It only took a year to turn things around again. John went into real estate.

When I finally sold the store in 1997, sales were just shy of a million dollars annually and I am proud of that. The town was still very small then and well under 10,000 people. I was also proud that I had done it on my own, with a great deal of help from my parents, of course. They had helped in the beginning years with their time and also with loans now and again. I did pay every penny back, at what I called loan shark rates.

One of the most stressful things in my life was selling the store. I spent so much of my youth there and it was like cutting off one of my arms, but I never looked back; I only think of it now and I wonder how I ever did it. The funny thing is that Julianna gave me a lecture last year on how I should have kept it for Danny and her. I am still glad I didn't. They have to find their own way in life.

I think that is all for the store era. I do have to go back to the relationships of then, as they were horrible for me, but not anymore tonight.. Now I am tired and I need to go to bed. I really need my beauty sleep tonight.

You know, I may be able to finish this soon and we can get closer to the present day, if I keep writing as much as I did tonight. The only problem is that the tough part has only just begun.

I love you and hope you have a good sleep too. I am anxious to find out if you are beginning to find what it is you are looking for in my words. Have you even had a glimpse of your ideal of me or should I have talked to the stove? I certainly have seen and heard my ideal of you. I will have to save that for yet another email. That one will be easy.

Good night
Irene

Sent: January 31, 2007 12:56 A.M.
Subject: Sick of emails yet?

It looks like I am still smoking. I just took my mother's house key and helped myself. They are still not home and I needed just one more before I go to sleep. I am under the impression that it helps me to relax. Maybe tomorrow I will quit.

I am taking my phone with me to bed, in case you decide to call or something.

Chapter 54

Sent: January 31, 2007 9:47 A.M.
Subject: I get to see you today!

I am not going into work today, other than a few minutes, this afternoon. I am going to stay home this morning, clean house and water plants. Maybe I will do a load of laundry at my mother's. They will be happy for my company.

I thought of another six pages that I could write to you, about something I touched on before, not in an email, but verbally and in person. It will have to wait until the end though. I need to deal with the rest of the relationships first. The last two before I married, probably had the most profound effects on me and in shaping who I was to become in life. It is not something I have shared with many others, other than my family and a few close friends. Maybe this is why it has taken me so long to get here.

Sal owned the large shipping company and was a number of years older than I was. As it turned out, he was a habitual cheater on his wife. He used to stop by the store for coffee all the time and one day, out of the blue, he made his pass. Our relationship turned from one of purely friendship, to lovers. It happened so fast; I didn't know what hit me and the next thing I knew he left her for me. I guess I was just such a sucker for, "I love you". I never lived with a man before, so this was a whole new experience for me.

I was now approaching thirty and the pressures and the need to give birth were starting to build. I think this was the real reason I allowed him into my life and believed all of his lies. Throughout my twenties, I was under the impression if I wasn't good enough to be a nun, then I would just get married and have six children. The only problem was that the closer I approached thirty, I started to reduce by one each year the number of children I could have.. By this time,

I didn't think there were many children left.

So here we were the happy couple. He actually left his company to his wife and came to work in the store. He and his wife never had children and he desperately wanted to have a family. I found out from his sister-in-law, months later when she came to check on me, that he had done this before. He wanted me pregnant as quickly as possible and I was happy to oblige and I was weeks late. He started to tell everyone we knew. Within two short weeks of this bliss and his eagerness to tell me where the crib should go, he went home for lunch one day and when he didn't return, I went to check. I found him and all of his belongings gone. I may as well have been hit by one of his trucks.

The first week I felt I had to do something about the suspected pregnancy. I hadn't seen my doctor yet so I didn't really know for certain. The last thing I wanted was a lifetime reminder of him and another abortion I couldn't go through. I bought a bottle of vodka, sat down one night and forced myself to drink as much of it as I could. It must have done the trick because by the next morning, I bled like never before. As far as everyone was concerned, I was never pregnant to begin with and it was never spoken about again, until now.

Over the weeks that followed, I sank deeper and deeper into depression; to the point that when I was driving I kept looking at the trees, thinking that if I could just hit one of them, then I could end it. This was in the middle of the recession and the store was generally quiet with a few customers coming in. As the days passed, it became more and more difficult for me to speak to anyone. I will never forget sitting there one day, thinking if I didn't open my mouth to speak soon, I would totally lose control of my mind and I would end up in some nut house.

I was sitting on my chair in the office and my foot kept going back and forth until I put a hole in the wall. Up until the time I sold the store, I insisted the hole never be patched as it would serve as a reminder of a place I never wanted to see again.

I was so far away in a blank space and so full of pain, it was unbearable. I remember praying for someone, anyone, to come into the store, so I would be forced to open my mouth and say something. In some way, this could save me from being lost forever and yet no one came.

I picked up the phone and dialed my mother and when she answered, I couldn't open my mouth to speak, except to tell her that I couldn't talk and I hung up. I continued to sit there swinging my foot and sinking deeper and deeper, wondering what it would be like to just run down the street screaming. I prayed to God to send someone in that would save me.

I thought I was ready to leave this world when a woman came into the store. It was a woman I had no tolerance for and she quite frequently came in.. I didn't like her because I viewed her as a simpleton and I had little patience for her. Now I found myself standing in front of her listening and, in my mind, all I wanted to do was to throw my arms around her and thank her for saving me. She pulled me back from the brinks of hell and after she left, I thanked God for sending her and I learned a huge lesson from the choice of the saviour He had sent.

The months of healing after that experience found me thanking God that I had survived and I spent the next few months in almost total solitude, except for the store. This is when I read the Bible, from cover to cover and every word. Since that time, I have never been remotely depressed about anything in life. I discovered, man may not love me, but God certainly did and He forgave me everything. It was at this time that I found new meaning in reasons to thank Him for my many blessings and even my painful experiences were actually blessings as well.

Jane from Buffalo's, reminds me of the woman who saved me that day. I know you think I don't like her and don't have tolerance for her. When I look at her, I see a great sadness and loneliness and I really wish someone would take her home and make her happy. I think she deserves it. She is the one who called me that day to join her in Banff for a coffee and I didn't go. I feel badly about that.

Now this was a difficult story to tell and I am glad it is over. I only have one more to go and I will be at the present, which is a much better place for me. I need to get dressed now and do some work. I hope the day flies by! If I get my work done, I may go on yet today. I am getting tired of dwelling in the past. What I would like to do is fill a book about all the happy thoughts and things I have done to make up for all I've written here. My life has been full of them and it certainly wasn't all pain and far from it.

I wonder what I will wear for you tonight. How can I show you how much I care? I'll think about that the rest of the day, until you arrive.

Love
Irene

Chapter 55

Sent: January 31, 1:22 P.M.
Subject: The Last One, I Promise

His name was David and he came into my life about the time I finished reading the Bible and I had forgiven myself and everyone around me. It would prove to be the second and last time I would pray for God to send a man for me to love and one who would love me back.

He was a mountain guide and, according to him, was living with a woman he was no longer in a relationship with. They owned the house together and they slept in separate bedrooms and shared the house merely for convenience. Needless to say, I was never invited over and I only once showed up unexpectedly during two years of being together. She was not home. Years later, when I was married, I ran into her and she confirmed to me that everything that he had said was true. I felt the pain even though John was next to me at the time.

He was Swiss and he had lost his mother at a very young age. Coincidentally, this was the same as the previous relationship. I have since read that men, who go through traumatic life experiences between the ages of nine to eleven, are to be avoided at all costs. I didn't know that at the time.

It was a very passionate relationship and something I never experienced before. It turned out to be my one and only "high altitude orgasm" in life. He was a pilot as well. I could spend an hour or more lightly touching his body from head to toe and none of the touching would be remotely related to sex. This came much later. I felt that what his body, mind and soul needed, was the energy mine easily gave off.. I remember lightly touching his fingers, each separately and then together and I could almost feel his body drawing out of me the energy or love he required. We spent many peaceful nights together like this. It got to a point where I couldn't even walk in front of his store without getting goose bumps. When I accidentally ran into him, my heart would speed up and my hands would become clammy. I would often switch to walking down the other side of the street in order to avoid him and his office.

The one thing that kept us apart was the woman living in his house. His story was something I wanted to believe, but my heart kept telling me "no". It was over two years that we had dated and he rarely asked me out for dinner and if you asked me what he gave me for birthdays or Christmas, I wouldn't be able to tell you. I don't recall receiving anything. He once took me to the car races in Calgary and an air show in Southern Alberta. I suppose I thought that my reward was the ability to give my love to him.

We took one vacation together and he flew me to Vernon to stay in a hotel and visit a girlfriend of mine and her husband. David was not a social person and he found it difficult. By the end of the night we fought and by morning, I found myself alone in the hotel room. He and his plane were gone. I phoned my girlfriend to pick me up. My girlfriend, her husband and I spent the next two days analysing it and we couldn't understand why. I came home on the Greyhound and that was my three day vacation for the year.

I gave up trying with him, but we continued to see each other. If he could torment me with thoughts of him living with another woman, I could be just as casual with the relationship. I started to see a DJ on a regular basis and another pilot from Calgary casually and all at the same time. I may have broken the heart of the DJ, but then I made it clear from the onset to both him and Ivan, that I was in love with David and that I was involved with the three of them. I made certain that David also knew about the other two.

I will never forget the day that David and I spent at the races. When we drove up to my house, the other pilot was sitting and waiting in front of my door. I told David, he could drop me at the corner. He noticed Ivan's vehicle and asked what I was worried about. I jumped out and he left.

I ended the interlude with the DJ and substituted him for John.

Not long after, I also ended the brief encounter with Ivan. He was ten years older than me and he was married to a woman ten years younger than me. Obviously, it didn't turn out well as he is the one that committed suicide a few years later. I am certain he was still in love with his childhood sweetheart.

A few months into dating John, I gave up on David and all the rest for good. I survived the relationships without getting depressed and I became a one-man woman again. John was divorced six months before we met and he continued to sow his wild oats for awhile. We know how this one ended.

Cephus, I love you very much and I do thank you for your patience. After many years, it has been good to get this poison out into the open where it belongs. I know it is difficult to listen to someone you love talk about their past relationships and I hope it doesn't upset you too much. This is the end of the past and I only look forward to the future now. I do hope you will not be one to point a finger at me. Please, remember the saying about, "every time you point a finger, there will be three pointing back at you".

Love
Irene

Part Eleven
Forgiveness

Chapter 56

Sent: January 31, 2007 10:24 A.M.
Subject: Back to Forgiveness

I just had a thought. I said I was never depressed since then and that isn't entirely true. These past couple of weeks have been very depressing for me, not even close to the same degree, but I have not felt this bad since then. I wasn't lying when I said to you that I actually had the thought that it would be better if I wasn't here. Now that thought, I never had during my eighteen year marriage, in spite of how "not" good it was.

The one thing I need to tell you is the way you look and think of me is very important. Right now, it seems that all your thoughts are so awful that it breaks my heart. Every bad thing you say about me, tears me apart inside. As much as I deserve it, I know it is not even close to who I really am.

I wake up each day, thinking today is the day you are going to see the light and forgive me and you don't. I know it takes time and you say you need and want proof of my love. I have been struggling to find what this proof is. How can I tell you? What is it I am supposed to say or do? There really are no words I can speak or write, because everything that flows from my mouth now, you think is a lie. The only answer I keep coming up with in my head about why I did what I did, is that I really didn't think you loved me and that I should just move on before my heart really gets broken again. I did not think you really cared for me and you won't believe that.

I hope you had a chance to look up the website I told you about

213

yesterday. You see, there is nothing I can say or do to make you forgive me. Forgiveness is something that you have to find in your own heart, because that is where it is. You are the only one who controls that and not me. I do know I will forgive you, if you can't find it in your own heart.

The one thing that will keep me sane and that will get me through this, is that I know God knows me, has kind thoughts for me, loves me and forgives me, even if, in the end, you won't. I will continue to thank Him for what I receive in life.

Today, I will thank Him for giving me you tonight.

Irene

Sent: January 31, 2007 11:58 A.M.
Subject: The past

Why even Mary Magdalene was forgiven. I can't help, but think that there is no way I have gained such power over your emotions in such a short period of time. Somehow, the infidelities of your other women have come back to haunt us.

I looked up the word, "infidelity", and the definition is "marital unfaithfulness". Could it be that you never truly forgave the first two and you still carry this? As a result, my cheating has carried three times the weight and has been more destructive to your emotions than if the other two had never happened. How much of this has to do with only me and the awful thing I have done? The first two relationships bore you three children which only add more pain and grief to a relationship when it ends.

You must be wondering why I said I would forgive you, if you couldn't find the forgiveness for me. I should maybe explain this. If you do not find it in your heart to forgive me, our relationship will end. I will be heartbroken and I will spend the rest of my days thinking that I found my soul mate and through this inability of yours to forgive, you rob us both of your ideal and mine. I do deserve to be forgiven and, if you can't, I forgive you.

Make sure that what is in your heart now, with all of its bitterness, is only about me and not someone else. Only then, do I have a chance to fix us, as I certainly will not be able to fix someone else's pain inflicted on you.

I love you very much and I will force myself not to write anymore this afternoon, as I want to be happy when you get here.

Love
Irene

Sent: January 31, 2007 5:59 P.M.
Subject: Deceitful and Dishonest

Dishonest: Disposed to lie or cheat
Deceitful: Intended to deceive or mislead

Cephus, these are the true meanings of those words and they really don't describe my character and they should not be used in the same sentence with my name. I did cheat on you one night, but I have not been dishonest or deceitful to you. I am not disposed to lie or cheat and I certainly have never intended to deceive or mislead you.

This is what the other women did to you by not telling you what they did in advance of you finding out. I, on the other hand, could not live with myself without being honest with you and, therefore, I told you. I began to see and feel your love for me and to hold this wrong -doing as a secret from you, did not fit my character. Am I not worthy of redemption and forgiveness of this act, because I chose not to hide it from you? I have begged for your forgiveness.

To tell me that I am lying when I say, I did not see or feel your love and that I knew all along what I was doing, is so totally unfair. If you reread all of those emails I sent to you between Christmas and New Year's, I clearly said, "many people love me both in the day and in the night and you are not one of them". Do you think I saw and felt your love when I wrote those words?

I am wondering which is better- whether for me to continue to speed through life with all of its work and pain or for you to take all the work and pain ever so slowly? It could be each of us needs to

215

change slightly to the opposite and there we could both be happier.

I love you and to think it is now 5:55 and in a couple of hours you will be here. I am so excited! It only took me three hours to get ready tonight. Joanna and even Gareth have been saying I am acting like a schoolgirl who has fallen in love for the very first time. Cynthia and the rest have been saying the same. Maybe I have.

Love for the first time!
Irene

Chapter 57

A number of weeks and so many words had passed, since the night of the betrayal and it did seem like we managed to resurrect the relationship from near death, but it was far from being easy. Most of the nights we spent together, were not pleasant, for either one of us. We wasted so much time in analyzing the "why", that we did actually stop living in the "now", as Cephus liked to call it, and we both hated it.

I think he thought because I was the cause of all this anguish that I possibly enjoyed it and was one of those women you meet in life, who love to make their men squirm. This was not me. He kept telling me over and over again, the person I had been in my past life was not a person he ever saw or knew and he wanted desperately to meet this good person. All he experienced, so far, was another woman who could have picked him up at any one of his million gigs and taken him home. This was not a woman he really ever wanted in his life, much less around his children. It took me a very long time to figure this out. All I could see was what was straight ahead and maybe my field of vision had totally diminished since my separation.

Most of those evenings, spent together, started with me in the morning in self analysis and looking in my mirror and then getting on with my normal day, which tended to be all over the place and very hectic. I often envisioned him, sitting out there somewhere at his keyboard or piano. He could be among a thousand people and I still could see him sitting there alone and lost in his music. He looked peaceful in his solitude, even though my betrayal caused him such grief. I still saw him this way and envied him for his still and very quiet soul. That was his life and was far from being mine. Since December, my life turned into such a waiting game, revolving around a new love, and I wondered where all the happiness of my new found freedom and love of me had gone since John had left. I could never seem to find a moment that I could call my own and maybe this is what truly separated us from really being together.

During these months, we fought quite often. At the end of my day, I would rush home to get ready for him at the very last minute and in haste. All I had time for was to shower, do my hair, shave my legs, do my make up and splash some perfume on. It reminded me of all those years of marriage. I managed to build up enough pent up energy in anticipation of him. I was generally nervous as hell waiting and counting the hours until he would arrive and I was generally exhausted, by the time he did. Before he would arrive, I would have a couple of drinks, in an attempt to slow me and my thoughts down. I likened it, to someone on speed, racing and I questioned how it is that we do slow down. He wanted me to live in the "now" and although, I knew what it meant, I didn't know how to fit it into my everyday life and busy schedule. During the course of the week, I would several times reread the emails that I had sent to make sure that it was still how I felt the next day and, not something whimsical. Somehow, they always seemed to make sense to me and they still do.

So often, during this time, we would start the night off fine and within an hour, one of us would say something to set the other off and we would be fighting. He would threaten to leave and often did, only to drive a block away and park. I would call him on his cell and apologize and he would drive back. Other times, I would take my key back and ask him to leave, but was thankful he never went far.

We would make love and then spend the whole morning talking and wondering what went wrong. All we knew was we loved each other. We were both trying to make it work and we forged ahead and continued to deal with our pain. For some reason, all my words, written during the course of the week, seemed to do nothing to stop him from hurting and I could see it in his eyes.

Chapter 58

Sent: February 1, 2007 7:12 P.M.
Subject: A Quiet Heart and Freedom

I actually wrote this a while back and had it scribbled on little bits of paper. All I have to do tonight is type it out. The only problem is I have to read it again. I have already written and said these thoughts many times to you before. Not to worry, as every time I sit down to write, I think of other things I need to say and the words keep popping out of my head and onto the paper.

What came to mind, this afternoon, was the thought again of this "all or nothing" and I wondered why I repeated this to you in so many emails over the months? I am almost sick of hearing it now. I asked myself: why would I want to accept someone into my life who was willing or possibly only capable of giving me half of himself? Was I prepared to accept and be satisfied with only half of a man?

This, I thought was a very good question and I revisited all of those past relationships, one more time. I discovered I was always satisfied with only half of all of them. Now here you are, also only willing to give me a small part of yourself.

I have watched you while you were playing and I have listened to you talk and I know that there is much more to you than you were giving me. I kept wanting and asking for more than just the superficial and you were not willing or prepared to give it.

You kept your whole other life, in Calgary, a total secret from me. My God, Cephus, right up until New Year's, I still thought, that there was a possibility you could be having a serious relationship with another woman in Calgary. You couldn't give me more because someone else in your life was getting the rest. Remember. I have never met your children and don't even know where you live, much less your home phone number and this is odd, to say the least.

219

At one point, I was even jealous that not me, but the clerks in the stores in Calgary saw you in the day. Only now, since the betrayal and my attempts to end this relationship, have I discovered that you are maybe willing to show and give me more of yourself. In the last three months, you seemed to be satisfied with only a small part of me and I kept hoping you would want more, but you didn't. You never asked me any questions. I kept trying to give you everything of myself, through my emails and although you loved to read them, you were never quite willing to share more of yourself.

I am too old now to settle for just half of you. I need and deserve all of someone. I have paid my dues in life with bad relationships. If I can't have all of someone now, I may as well treat this relationship like a fling because that is really all it becomes, if your whole heart is not in it. I know how to do this and I proved it in January. Unfortunately, all those bad relationships in my past have made me very good at it, but it certainly is not the sum of who I am or want to be.

Please remember, I am the chameleon and, in order to protect myself, I will change to suit my surroundings. If I don't think you care for me, I will look elsewhere and pretend also I don't care. On the other hand, if I see and know, in my heart, that you do care, then heaven and earth could not stand in my way. Being faithful to someone is a very easy thing to do in life and I have never had a problem with this.

Maybe what I needed from you and didn't get, was a total commitment to our relationship and instead, I only received a half. In return, you only receive a half a commitment from me, as well.

Now I find out that this brick wall you have erected, was a result of someone else screwing around on you and here I go and do the same thing. To break your heart was not a purposeful and vindictive decision on my part. In fact, if you had opened your life up to me, including meeting your children, I guarantee you that I would not have done what I did.

I have bared my soul to you almost right from the beginning, through my emails and, until Marley at the Bison, what I got in return was only bits and pieces of your soul.. I was always led to believe that black people had a lot of soul, but I wasn't seeing much of yours and this was an unexpected disappointment to me.

This constant pouring out of my heart, costs a great deal of emotion. I lost another five pounds this past week and I haven't even gone to a gym. I want to stop talking and writing for awhile; and yes, it did hurt to find out you had destroyed all of my emails after my betrayal. None of those words were lies. What you did was take the gift of my soul and threw it away. Think for a minute; it was a powerful blow to your heart that erected that brick wall of yours and quite likely it was going to take one of equal or greater force, to knock it all down again. You know, you should be thanking God it is down now. You can actually get on with your life and with a wide open heart. This way, you can accept a new love, with all of your heart and not a guarded one or a half of one.

Think of how much better that new relationship could be, as a result. The beauty of it is; it doesn't have to be with me and someone who has cheated on you and it can be with anyone you choose. Who knows? You may even enjoy your music more as a result of this new freedom.

I love you and I must get back to being happy and a quiet heart. I hope you will never get tired of....knocking on someone's door.

All my love
Irene

P.S. Maybe this is what the world needs, is an Open Heart?